SAMUEL
The Seer
First In The Prophetic Movement In Israel

Other Biblical Character Studies by Walter C. Kaiser, Jr.

The Lives and Ministries of ELIJAH and ELISHA

ABRAHAM The Friend of God

JOSHUA A True Servant Leader

JOSEPH From Prison to Palace

The Journey from JACOB to Israel

NEHEMIAH The Wall Builder

SAMUEL   The Seer
First In The Prophetic Movement In Israel

———✡———

Coming Soon

DAVID A Man After God's Own Heart

MOSES The Man Who Saw the Invisible God

SOLOMON The King with a Listening Heart

THE TWELVE The "Minor" Prophets Speak Today

ZECHARIAH The Quintessence of Old Testament Prophecy

DANIEL The Handwriting is on the Wall

RUTH The Moabite and the Providence of God
and
ESTHER God Preserves the Jewish Nation

SAMUEL

The Seer

First In The Prophetic Movement In Israel

Walter C. Kaiser, Jr.

Lederer Books
an imprint of
Messianic Jewish Publishers
Clarksville, MD 21029

Cover Design by Lisa Rubin,
Messianic Jewish Publishers
Graphic Design by Yvonne Vermillion,
MagicGraphix.com
Editing by George A. Koch,
copyedit.pro

1   2022
ISBN 978-1-951833-29-9

Printed in the United States of America

Published by:
Lederer Books
An imprint of
Messianic Jewish Publishers
6120 Day Long Lane
Clarksville, MD 21029

Distributed by:
Messianic Jewish Publishers & Resources
Order line: (800) 410-7367
lederer@messianicjewish.net
www.MessianicJewish.net

To
President Barry Corey and his wife Paula,
Genuine Yokefellows with us in the work of the Gospel
At Gordon-Conwell Theological Seminary,
Now at BIOLA University and Talbot Seminary.
And To
Their son Samuel, whom I had the privilege
Of dedicating to the Lord.

Table Of Contents

Lesson 1
God Makes Good His Word
1 Samuel 1:1–2:10

Some incidents in the Bible just seem too small and without widespread or enough general merit to include in a book with such cosmic range of implications as the Holy Scripture. But the story of the birth of the future prophet Samuel is more than worth its space, once one becomes aware of how significant this transitional character was to the history of Israel's future, for he is at once both the fountainhead for the line of prophets who were to follow, and the one who installed Israel's first king in a royal line that stretched from 1150 B.C. to 586 B.C.E. Both of those achievements were part of no small accomplishments by the power of God.

Samuel, therefore, seems to be at the head of a long line of non-writing prophets in Scripture, for by the time the biblical narrative arrives at the books of 1 and 2 Kings, it becomes obvious that what otherwise seems to be a set of historical books really centers on a string of prophets sent by the Lord. This is why the books of Joshua, Judges, Samuel and Kings are called the "former Prophets" in the Jewish canon. Thus, some ten prophets or prophetesses are named in 1 and 2 kings: Nathan (1 Kings 1:5–53); Ahijah (11:26–40); an unnamed prophet from Judah in northern Israel's King Jeroboam I (13:1–32); Micaiah's ministry to King Ahab about his pending death in the battle he is to enter (22:5–28); Isaiah's word to King Hezekiah that he will be given 15 more years of life (2 Kings 18-20); the prophetess Huldah's explanation to King Josiah of the meaning of the newly found book of the Law of Moses (22:14–20); along with other lesser-known prophets such as Shemiah, Jehu, Jonah and the well-known and hallmark ministries of Elijah and Elisha, spanning 1 Kings 16:20 to 2 Kings 11:20, not to mention the "sons of the prophets" schools Samuel must have had a hand in forming at this time as well.

Our text in Samuel, however, begins innocently enough with a family at home in the Ephraimite hill country, in a town called Ramathaim (meaning "double heights"), where a certain Elkanah, who surprisingly (given the teaching of Scripture) had two wives, Peninnah and Hannah. Peninnah was having children as fast as popping popcorn, but Hannah was barren and without even one child (v. 2b), because the Lord had closed her womb (v. 5b). To say the least, this caused a lot of agitation and friction between the two women! However, barren women often were the very instruments God would use in the history of redemption, as seen in the lives of Sarah, Rebekah, Rachel, Manoah's unnamed wife, and on into New Testament times. But this only goes to show that our helplessness and hopelessness present no barrier to the Lord; often our inability only becomes the precise opportunity for God's starting point, which leaves the credit for what is done to God's grace and mercy, and not to our own efforts and work. So, just when we think we are without strength or resources, or think we are even in charge of our own ways in the events of life, our Lord moves in to show himself to be the strong Son of God as he had promised in his word. Let us watch this very development of things in the life of a young Samuel.

By Silencing Unfair Taunts Against Us – 1:1–8

A Certain Man

Elkanah, son of Tohu, son of Zuph, was not overly noteworthy compared to the better-known mortals of that day, but he was chosen by the Lord, who was now calling him for a special task. Elkanah was a Levite (1 Chronicles 6:26-27, 34-35), and his ancestor Zuph was a descendant of the line of Kohath, whose sons took care of the Ark of God (Numbers 3:31). But when this story, recorded here, was narrated, he was not involved in any Levitical duties. Still, he went each year to each of the three mandatory feasts the people of Israel celebrated, along with his two wives, Hannah and Peninnah.

A Certain Woman

It was clear that Hannah was Elkanah's favorite wife, even though she was not able to have any children. Her rival, of course, was Peninnah, who apparently took every opportunity to rub in the fact of Hannah's infertility, to her great discomfort. One could just imagine the conversation around Elkanah's dinner table. Perhaps it went something like this:

"Mommy, why doesn't Aunt Hannah have any children?"

(Peninnah acts surprised as if she had not heard the question, but clearly pleased with the question from her child, replies only too gladly.) "What did you ask, dear?" (She indeed has heard, but for her this was but another occasion to make Hannah feel uncomfortable and distressed over her barrenness and to rub into her soul the sore of her infertile condition.)

"I said, why isn't Aunt Hannah having children? Doesn't she want some?"

"Oh, yes, she dearly wants to have children, but ... well, Hannah, what shall I tell my children? You answer them for me." (With this type of constant haranguing and irritation, Hannah once again flees from the table, weeping and sobbing painfully.)

"Oh well, we must not pry, children; it only makes Hannah cry! ... Oh, by the way, Hannah," she shouts to her in the next room, "did I tell you that I'm pregnant again? I'm sure you are very happy for me!"

Day after day, and time after time, Peninnah must have baited Hannah with such talk that was hard for her rival to swallow. But this agitation drove Hannah to talk and cry out to the Lord all the more. Deliverance, if it was to come from any source, must certainly come from the Living God.

By Answering the Prayers of Our Desperation – 1:9–18

Hannah's Prayer

Year after year, as the feasts were celebrated at the house of God in Shiloh at the appointed time, Hannah would refuse to eat anything at the feast, for her heart was too heavy to enjoy any food. Instead, she poured out her heart "in [the] bitterness of [her] soul]" (v. 10a).

Now Eli, the priest, who routinely sat on a designated chair (called the "Seat of Moses") near the door of the Lord's house, observed how Hannah wept and was very heavy-hearted. He mistook her actions as a clear sign of drunkenness (vv. 13–14), so he decided to rebuke her for her lack of sobriety (an act of rebuking he might well have practiced on correcting his delinquent sons, whom he had decidedly and consistently failed to reprove), but Hannah quickly cleared up the misconception that she was inebriated for the High Priest Eli, who had continued to upbraid her. She informed him she had been praying to the Lord; she was not at all drunk! Notice the use of silent prayer in ancient Israel from the heart of an individual!

In fact, Hannah vowed to the Lord that if God would give her a son, she would give him back to the Lord to serve him in the house of God all the days of his life (v. 11). Note how free Hannah was to go directly to God in prayer. Her freedom of access surprises us, but it does not surprise God, who has always invited all to come to him in prayer. She went directly to the throne of grace—as direct an access to the Lord as any in our day can go to God in prayer. Her prayer illustrated how fervent she was (v. 10), how specific she was (v. 11) and how she would persevere until God acted on her behalf.

Eli's Blunder

As mentioned, Eli had repeatedly not rebuked his own sons for their great wickedness of having sex with women in the tabernacle (2:22–25), yet when he thought he saw sin in other people, he apparently was quick to judge and rebuke them—especially on what may have been one of his favorite topics: drunkenness! Hannah answered quickly affirmed that she was not inebriated; her misery came from the sorrow of her heart.

Eli quickly shifted from his rebuke of Hannah to one of bestowing on her God's favor and blessing (v. 18). With this assurance, she went on her way and finally ate some food at the festival, for she believed God's answer was on the way. No longer was she downcast (v. 18). God had promised with his word, and that was good enough for her. The promises of God have always had such a healing effect on all who would trust him. This effectiveness and power of the word of God is a key factor to note in this text.

By Granting Us Gifts to Return to Him – 1:19–28

The Theology of Remembrance

When God remembers someone or something, it means more than he merely called that person or thing to his mind; it means God also had decisively *acted* on behalf of that person or request. In Western thought, we tend to separate the thought from the action itself, but this was not so in the ancient Near East. Literally the verse in Hebrew goes this way:

> "Yahweh gave me my *asking*, which I *asked* from him; and I also have given back what was *asked* of Yahweh, all the days he lives, he is the one that is *asked* for from Yahweh." (vv. 20c, 27–28; my literal translation)

Thus, when God remembered Hannah, it was not like when we suddenly remember something and slap our foreheads as we say to the person to whom we had made a promise we had been forgotten: "I'm sorry, I forgot all about it." Instead, when we remember the Lord and his suffering for us at the Lord's table, known as the Eucharist, we are not simply to call to mind a hill, roughly in the shape of a skull, with three crosses on it, and then say: "There, we have remembered the Lord's death and his atonement for us." Rather, such remembering calls for appropriate *actions* on our part—after all ADONAI has done for us, actions that show we appreciate all that was done on our behalf.

The Theology of Asking

When Hannah received the answer to her prayers as a son was born to her, she named him "Samuel, saying, 'Because I *asked* the LORD for him'" (v. 20). However, Samuel's name in fact means "the name of God." But since the words "from Yahweh" are emphatic in Hebrew, the primary point of Hannah's joy was that her son was a *gift* "from God (Yahweh)," who had now opened her womb. So Hannah had played on the Hebrew words meaning to "ask [from] God" (*shoal* + *'el*) and the form "name of God" (which in Hebrew is *shem* + *'el*), i.e., "Samuel."

After she had weaned Samuel, who would have been about three years old in that culture, she brought him, as she had promised, to the house of the Lord with "a three-year-old bull" (this is confirmed by a reading in the Dead Sea Scrolls, as well as the Greek translation and the Syriac version), along with three-fifths of a bushel of flour (though cf. Numbers 15:9), and a skin of wine" (v. 24).

Four times Hannah uses the word "to ask," as that reflects v. 17, where Eli the priest said, "May the God of Israel grant you what you have *asked* of him." Thus God's gift to Hannah was made over to God for his full use as he pleased.

Samuel was destined to become one of *ADONAI*'s key prophets; indeed, he is sort of the forerunner of a whole line of prophets that will follow him.

By Manifesting His Control Over Our Times – 2:1–10

The Theme of Hannah's Prayer

The theme of Hannah's beautiful prayer in 1 Samuel 2:1–10 is summarized in verse 10c: "The LORD will judge the ends of the earth." Moreover, ten times her prayer in these ten verses focuses not on herself, as so often we moderns tend to do in our praying, but instead focuses on the poor, the feeble, the barren and the ungodly. Her prayers, then, were centered on others and the work of God in his wrap-up of history.

In the great finale, which is the day of God's judgment (2:9–10), our Lord will accomplish a great deal through his anointed One, the Messianic King, who is to come. This terminology is very similar to God's judging the ends of the earth, as it is found in Psalms 2 and 110. God "will thunder against them [the wicked] from heaven (v. 10b).

The Jewish *Targum* understood part of verse 10 thus: And "exalting the horn of his Anointed, he will magnify the kingdom of his Messiah." No wonder Acts 3:24 claimed: "All the prophets from Samuel on ... foretold these days," i.e., the days when Messiah would come to earth a second time. Yes, God did thunder forth his lightning on the Philistines at the battle of Mizpah, but that was only a small foretaste of what it would be like on the day when Messiah would thunder in a way that the whole world would be aware of his climactic act of judgment before he returned to earth once again.

Hannah's Own Personal Testimony – 2:1–3

Repeatedly Hannah uses the personal pronouns "my" and "I" to indicate her experience and her own confession of faith. Surprisingly, she does not direct her barbs directly at Peninnah, for the first two verbs in these verses are plural, as is the word "your." Thus, it was framed as a general warning against all proud boasters that they must give praise to *ADONAI* alone.

Hannah's General Statement – 2:4–9

God remains the dominant person in Hannah's prayer. What Hannah had experienced was once again just a mere sample of the way God would intervene on behalf of all who trusted him and waited for his deliverance even up to the last day. Moreover, every time each of us experiences the deliverance of God, it is but a down payment on the full deliverance that is to come as his kingdom comes into its fullness one day in the future.

Conclusions

1. Some may complain: "So what's the big deal? Hannah now has a son, so things should be settling down in the house of Elkanah in the hills of Ephraim. But there is an enormously big deal, in case any missed it: Here is the scale model of how God works, and here is the way Messiah will come and judge all persons as he concludes history in the last days!

2. Every time a believer is lifted up out of the bogs of their distress, it is but a sample of the full deliverance we are certain will come when our Lord returns once again.

3. Opposition to others may seem so trivial to us, but it may ultimately be that the opposition aimed against others is also directed against the Lord himself. So beware!

4. The act of remembrance is more than a cognitive act, for it requires us to act on the basis of what we have called to mind.

Lesson 2

The Power of the Word of God

1 Samuel 3:1–4:1a

On October 31, 1517, a little-known Augustinian monk by the name of Martin Luther posted his *Ninety-five Theses* on the Castle Church door in Wittenberg, Germany. Luther had used the newly published Greek New Testament, prepared by Erasmus, to render the Greek word *metanoiete* as "repent" instead of "do penance." That is what probably started it all.

This translation work by Luther had been preceded by John Wycliffe's new translation of the Bible, the fiery sermons of Savonarola in Florence, Italy, and the martyrdom of John Huss in Constance, Germany. Luther's bold move was followed by the ministries of John Calvin, Ulrich Zwingli, Menno Simons, and John and Charles Wesley. For these men, the dominant theme of their work was *Sola Scriptura*, meaning, "Scripture alone" was the word of God. This too formed the dominant theme of the passage we will examine here, 1 Samuel 3:1–4:1a.

There also was another motto that came from Geneva, Switzerland: "After darkness, light." This meant that through the preaching of God's Word, light would come to God's people and lift the darkness of ignorance of the gospel of grace and salvation. Therefore, six sermons a week were prescribed for the people of that day according to the ordinances of the Church of Geneva in 1541 C.E.: a sermon at dawn on Sunday, another at 9:00 A.M., catechism for children at noon on Sunday, another sermon at 3 P.M., and three more on Monday, Wednesday and Friday. But a warning against neglecting the power of God's Word had already been given as far back as the text Solomon gave in Proverbs 29:18, which championed the view that "Where there is no vision [i.e., any input of revelation from God], the people perish [i.e., they become ungovernable.]" It is this power and effectiveness in the life of society and the Church we will now examine in this text.

God Can Make His Word Scarce – 3:1

It Is Rare in Its Exposure to the People

God had withdrawn his revelation and his message from the people because they wanted what they wanted—which was not his word! It was not part of their desires. The possession of God's word was no small favor or treasure to God's people, if only they would recognize it. The gift of his word was second only to the coming gift of his Son in his personal, incarnate form, to be with us for those approximately thirty years of life on earth.

Therefore, because of the sinful habits and attitudes of the people, God had made his Word scarce so that only a hungry few who really sought it out could find it. Individuals could not manufacture, manipulate, duplicate it or substitute anything for that powerful word from God. Only the Lord could give his word to the people. It could not be artificially aroused and stimulated solely by increasing the number of those graduating from our schools in our culture, or from those of the prophets in Samuel's day. In fact, the scarcity of God's word was a sign of God's judgment on sin, especially in this case where there existed a corrupted priestly leadership, and a people who were starving because of a famine for hearing the word of God (cf. Amos 8:11).

It Is Rare in Its Effect

As noted, Amos 8:11–12 confirmed this low estimate of the word, for later in Israel's history, God would announce a famine, only this time it would not be a famine of bread or water but a famine for hearing the Word of the Lord. It seems that most of the world today is in one of those same periods where there again is a "famine for [not] hearing the Word of God"; thus, instead on doing consistent expositions of the biblical text, wherein we study God's Word verse after verse and chapter after chapter, topics of one's own choosing are substituted instead for teaching what the Scriptures themselves say. We must repent of the absence of our delight, hunger and joy for hearing and doing of the whole of the Word of God as well as examine it in all its detail. Biblical poverty is an alarming state for all too many persons even in our day, but it is one of the most awful pandemics that can visit any nation.

Sometimes God just gives us what we want, but as a result he thereby also sends leanness to our souls as well (Psalm 106:15; 74:3–9). Thus, when God grows silent, the darkness from the absence of the Word of God among us increases, and so does the depth of our gloom and sadness. As the Church has moved away from preaching the Word and substituted other activities *in its place*, such as musical entertainment, dance and other surrogates to evoke an emotional response, it has given in to the agenda of the age. Scripture must be put back in its rightful central and dominant place with the pulpit back in the center of the platform and the Word of God prominently proclaimed.

God Can Make His Word Startling 3:2–14

His Word Is Startling in Its Call

God himself breaks the silence of the previous years of famine of the Word by issuing or a "call" in verses 4–10 some eleven times. In the meantime, Eli was losing his physical eyesight, but even more tragically, he was also losing his spiritual eyesight. It was young Samuel's task to make sure the lamp of God had not gone out in the Tabernacle. God had providentially provided the young boy Samuel through Hannah's prayers for a child.

Verse 7 says Samuel "did not yet know the LORD," so should we conclude that he was so dull and dimwitted that he did not recognize God's call? No! God does not blame Samuel in this passage for failing to immediately heed his call; but God explained that such was the state of religion, that religious affections and teachings were so low that even a boy raised in the house of God was ignorant of his person and work. We too must not play down the significance of teaching the youngest of our children, for it is at this time that habits and affections are formed!

But note a fact that is just as important: the tenderness, kindness and gentleness of the Lord. He does not berate Samuel for being what might seem to be his failure to know the Lord who was speaking to him. God merely kept coming to Samuel and standing there, waiting for him to respond. How magnificent of the God of all glory and grace—that he should be "standing" there, "waiting," and still "calling" a mere mortal—and a young lad at that!

It Is Startling in Its Content

God's word may involve not only good news, but bad news as well. His word in this case was so startling in its words of judgment that it would make the ears of all who heard it "tingle" (cf. Habakkuk 1:5). The message from the Lord was this: Judgment would come to the house of Eli because he had refused to rebuke his sons for the sins he knew about (1 Samuel 2:27–29). His sons had "blasphemed" the Lord (3:13; some Hebrew texts and the Septuagint actually use this exact word).

Here is the tension many of God's servants are under when they are called to deliver the word of God. Some of his messengers merely smooth God's people with comfort, never getting around to telling them about their sin and the forgiveness that lies ahead for all who repent. Other messengers only preach judgment, with very little comfort, encouragement or concern for the people being addressed. God's messengers must have a high regard for both the truth of God (even when it is about judgment) and the comfort that also comes from God. They must afflict the comfortable and comfort the afflicted, as the old saying goes!

God's Word Is Sovereign Over Us – 3:15–18

There Is Often a Natural Fear to Announce Judgment

This is why Samuel was afraid to tell Eli what God had told him (3:15), for he knew it was a message of judgment aimed at Eli's family because their father had not rebuked his sinful boys in their roles as priests. But when Eli called him to learn what God had spoken to him the night before, he told Samuel, "Do not hide it from me. May God deal with you (be it ever so severely), if you hide from me anything he told you" (v. 17). That is, if Samuel decided to pull his punches and hold back some of the harsh details of what God had told him, the judgment might also fall and rest on Samuel's head for telling only part of what God had said, but not the part about the judgment that was coming to Eli and his sons. What an awesome warning this is to God's messengers today! We must not pick and choose what we will tell the people of God, proclaiming only happy news! We are given no freedom to doctor-up or smooth-out what God's word teaches; it must be given straightforwardly, the truth and nothing but the truth!

There Is an Acknowledgement That God Is Sovereign

When Eli heard the message God told Samuel, Eli merely said, "He is the LORD" (v. 18). God's people in that day, and in our day, are to say "Amen" to God's judgments as well as his "blessings" (e.g., Deuteronomy 28). Moreover, if God does not judge evil, then eventually (if not sooner) all good and righteousness will get discouraged. So Eli continued, "Let [God] do what is good in his eyes" (v. 18).

God's Word Secures the Servants He Sends – 3:19-4:1a

Nothing Spoken by God's Servants Will Fall to the Ground

God later promised the prophet Isaiah the same thing as he now told Samuel, for when he said in Isaiah 55:11 that his word would never come back to his servants "empty," but that it would accomplish that for which it was sent, our Lord gave an important promise that would be true in all generations. This is why Charles Spurgeon, that great British pulpiteer of yesteryear, warned that the moment the Church of God despised the teachings of the pulpit, God would despise her as well. There is no substitute for the honest exposition of the Word of God as the center of our worship services and our daily devotions.

Everyone Knew That Samuel Was Accredited as a Prophet of God

This raises the question: What is it that really validates our ministries for the Lord? Is it the growth in the physical plant of the Church? Is it the growth in the number of people coming to our services? Is it the growth of the Church budget and the income numbers of the amount of giving to the Church? Is it not the best measure of the effectiveness of any work for God to be evaluated on the way the Word of God is taught and preached and the way lives of the listeners are changed by the power of that word?

Acclaim from the media, as well as the focusing of the spotlight on the opinions of the community, are not reliable indicators of God's validation. The best gauge of the effectiveness of the preaching of God's Word is in how relevant and effective by the results it produces in the lives of its hearers (4:1a). There is no substitute for real, genuine change in lives of the listeners to the Word of God than that so abundantly produced from the powerful effects on hearing his Word.

Conclusions

1. If Light is ever to come to our present darkness, it will only come through the preaching of the Word of God. For too long now, too many have sat in darkness, languishing in hopes that faithful exposition of the Word of God would come into their lives.

2. We must be attentive to the call of God and declare his Word fearlessly and compassionately to this present dark world.

3. Where a culture of people is devoid of the revelatory Word of God, that culture goes crazy and soon gets out of hand and becomes ungovernable and out of control (cf. Exodus 34:25).

4. We mortals do not live by bread alone, but by every word that comes from the mouth of God.

Lesson 3

Presuming on the Presence of God
1 Samuel 4:1–22

1 Samuel 4:1a has concluding remarks on chapter 3, which deals with Samuel's call. In effect, it draws a heavy line across the biblical history, for we will not hear any more of Samuel again until the revival breaks out in chapter 7. But for the time being, we must teach some "Ark-eology" lessons; the "Ark of the Covenant" takes center stage in 1 Samuel 4–6.

The Hebrew text, which most English translations follow, seems to imply Israel was the aggressor in the battle that ensued, but the Greek Septuagint seems to preserve a longer original text that makes the Philistines the initiating aggressors in this battle. The LXX read in part: "It happened at that time that the Philistines mustered [their army] to fight Israel and Israel went out…" In fact, this omission from the Hebrew text may have resulted because of what is called haplography, i.e., an omission that occurs because the eye of the scribe copying this text slipped from the first occurrence of the verb for "went out" (in v. 1a) to the second in v. 1b. Regardless, Israel was forced into combat as a result of what seems to have been a Philistine prior attack.

The problem this text deals with is the fact that Israel experienced an overwhelming defeat somewhere in the uninhabited area between the towns of Ebenezer and Aphek (1b, 2). Aphek was just twenty miles north of Ekron, the northernmost city of the famous Philistine *pentapolis* ("five cities") in the Sharon Plains. The other four cities in this Philistine group were Ashdod, Ashkelon, Gaza and Gath. The site of Ebenezer seems to have gained its name after a victory Israel experienced there a little later in 1 Samuel 7:12.

That Our God Will Always Be Present for Us – 4:1–4

Israel was terribly surprised when they were so thoroughly routed by the Philistine army (4:2). The people of God had gotten so accustomed to being helped and aided by the Lord in battle that for them the unthinkable had happened. Four thousand Israeli soldiers had lost their lives on the battlefield. But the question was, why?

This led the "elders" (v. 3), who asked when the troops had returned back to camp: "Why did the LORD bring defeat upon us today before the Philistines?" But one wonders why the threats Moses had taught them in Leviticus 26:17 and Deuteronomy 28:25 had not come to their minds and caused the nation to repent before they went out into battle and before God's judgment arrived.

> I will set my face against you [the LORD had warned], so that you will be defeated by your enemies [if you turn away from me]. (Leviticus 26:17)

> The LORD will cause you to be defeated before your enemies. You will go at them from one direction, but flee from them in seven, and you will become a thing of horror to all the nations on earth. (Deuteronomy 28:25)

They knew, of course, that it was the Lord who was doing the work of opposing them, but they still missed the point as to why he was doing it. They asked, "Why did the Lord bring defeat on us?", but they just let the question hang out there. It was time for self-examination and a time when the question was meant to bother them and help them to spring into an appropriate action that was pleasing to God.

Instead of responding personally in confession and repentance, they brainstormed an idea of their own: *Let's get the Ark of the Covenant and take it into battle the next time. Surely that will mean God will be forced to defend his own honor, prestige and people!* It was a way of trying to force God's hand, or twisting his arm, as it were. Moreover, it also was a type of "rabbit's-foot theology" that said, *Instead of exercising faith in*

God, we'll use the Ark as a talisman, or good-luck charm, for things to go our way. In that case, superstition had surely replaced faith, and God's word was forgotten.

The Ark of the Covenant was a box 3.75 feet by 2.25 feet wide and high. It was always kept in the Tabernacle, behind the veil that separated the Holy of Holies from the Holy Place. This is where it was kept, unless Israel was on the move marching in the wilderness. The Ark stood for God's rulership, for its full name was "The Ark of the Covenant of the LORD of Hosts [Almighty], [who is] enthroned on the cherubim" (4:4). But it also stood for the revelation of what the Ark contained, for inside it was stowed the two tablets with the Ten Commandments written on them. The Ark also stood for the place of reconciliation between God and man, for on top of this sacred box was the "mercy seat," where once each year, at the time of Yom Kippur, the blood of the slain goat was sprinkled on this mercy seat, symbolizing the atonement God would make available to all who believed (Leviticus 16). Finally, the Ark was also a sign of God's guidance and leading them, as it certainly had in the wilderness pilgrimage (Numbers 10:35), and it was most prominently used at the Jordan River crossing in Joshua 3–4, and later at the conquest of Jericho (Joshua 6:6–7:25).

All of this illustrates how a little knowledge is sometimes a dangerous thing. Israel remembered how God fought for them when the Ark was present, but they wrongly thought that box was invested with some sort of magic, for as a result of a relaxed preaching of the Word of God, they had by this time forgotten how their hearts had previously been more attuned to God in faith and repentance in those former times. In this way, it is possible for our own contemporary leaders (similar to the "elders") to misuse their knowledge of the past and thus succeed in deluding themselves, and those they lead, about the real state of spirituality of our lives. They had forgotten that the difference was not in the presence of the Ark, but in the condition of the people's hearts and the genuineness of their obedience.

That We May Substitute Religious Symbols for Holy Living – 4:5–11

When the Ark appeared in the battle, a huge cry and cheer went up (v. 5), which turned out to be a lot of worked-up bravado, for it gave only a momentary hope of victory. Israel was confusing an outward form of real faith in God with the genuine article. These shouts of overwhelming confidence in the Israelite camp did, however, for the moment arouse deep consternation in the enemies' camp (vv. 6–8), for the Philistines were not all that unfamiliar with Israel's history and what God had done on their behalf in past battles at the Red Sea, or with the two kings in Transjordania, or even in the conquest of the land of Canaan. But this was all hype and a lot of bravado on the part of the people, and it offered no assurance of success in the battle Israel was facing. The Philistines were indeed afraid:

> "A god has come into the camp. We're in trouble! Who will deliver us from the hand of these mighty gods? They are the gods who struck the Egyptians with all kinds of plagues in the desert. Be strong, Philistines! Be men, or you will be subject to the Hebrews, as they have been to you. Be men, and fight." (vv. 7–9)

But as it turned out, it was Israel that got struck down and totally defeated, not the Philistines (v. 10), and every man fled to his own tent. Worse still, the Ark of God was captured by this heathen nation (v. 11a), and Eli's two sons, who were transporting the Ark, were wounded in battle and died (v. 11b).

Ralph Davis, in his commentary on this chapter, makes two observations worth repeating here: "[God] will suffer shame rather than allow you to carry on a false relationship with him," and [God] will allow you to be disappointed with him if it will awaken you to the sort of God he really is."[1]

All of this raises the question in our lives: What is it that motivates us for all that we do for Christ? Is it that things go better with tithing?

---

1. Dale Ralph Davis, *Looking on the Heart: Expositions on the Book of I Samuel, Volume 1* (Grand Rapids: Baker Books, 1994), 53.

We sing "Thou art worthy!", but do we really mean, "Thou art *useful*"? This calls for some real soul-searching, which does not mean we drop some or all of these practices, but we must ask: First of all, what is the condition of our hearts?

That We May Count On the Fact That the Threatened Judgment Will Not Come On Us – 4:12-22

On the same day the Ark of God was captured and Eli's sons Hophni and Phinehas died in battle, a Benjamite messenger ran from the battle line to bring the news to the city of Shiloh, where the Tabernacle temporarily was. His clothes were torn and he had dust on his head. He hurriedly told those in the city what had happened in the battle, causing a great shriek to go up from the whole city (v. 13d). The priest Eli, now 98 years of age, blind, and quite heavy, was sitting on his usual chair by the side of the road, watching and waiting for news from the battle that had been underway, for he greatly feared for the Ark of God (v. 13a–b). When he heard the noise from the town, he asked, "What is the meaning of the uproar?" (v. 14). The Benjamite hurried over to Eli and reported, "I have just come from the battle line; I fled from it this very day" (v. 16).

Eli pressed, "What happened, my son?" (v. 16b). Then Eli heard the heavy news: "Israel has fled before the Philistines, the army has suffered heavy losses, your two sons Hophni and Phinehas are dead, and the ark of God has been captured" (v. 17). The last part of the calamity—the news of the ark—was too much for Eli. He fell over backwards off his chair, broke his neck and instantly died (v. 18).

Eli had been warned already about his sons' bad conduct (2:27–34, 3:12–14), but he did not take the action he should have as a father and a spiritual leader of the people. Thus their judgment was not a surprise to Eli, but the capture of the Ark was too overwhelming. How could God let his own honor and dignity suffer such humiliation in front of such raw pagans? But what Eli, and perhaps his fellow Israelites, along with the Philistines thought might be the lasting shame of God, instead became the very means on the very same day in which God began to restore his name and reputation in front of all who had come to the opposite conclusion.

One more event took place that day. Phinehas' wife suddenly went into labor, and she bore a son just as the news was arriving of the capture of the Ark and the news of the death of her husband and her father-in-law (v. 19). As she was dying, she named her newborn son Ichabod, saying, "The glory has departed from Israel" (v. 21), referring to the Ark of God. What she said, however, was more than just a mere saying, for in reality, God's presence and glory were now gone away from Israel, and it was time for Israel to wake up, repent and return to the Lord (v. 22).

Conclusions

1. It is a real tragedy when God no longer will dwell / abide with his people because of their sin!

2. Over how many homes, churches, countries of the world has God had to declare in our times the word "Ichabod," i.e., the "glory has departed"? Only a turning back to the Lord will change that indictment.

3. From Psalms 78:59–64 and Jeremiah 7:12, we learn that Shiloh, the place where the Tabernacle was kept, was subsequently plundered and destroyed.

4. God will not be put off by substitutes and artificial symbols that presume on his presence in place of his powerful presence and Word.

Lesson 4

Toying with the Sanctity of the Lord
1 Samuel 5:1–7:1

As a background to appreciating the events that follow in chapters 5–7, we need to first get an appreciation for who the Philistines were, for they became Israel's main nemesis during this period. The name "Philistine" was represented in Egyptian royal texts as *prst*, and it begin to appear around 1185 B.C.E. as part of the invading "Sea Peoples." Some two centuries prior, however, they appear in the Egyptian Amarna Letters (ca. 1400 B.C.E.) as a small group of settlers in the Gaza area during the Patriarchal Era. Apparently, they had migrated from Asia Minor by way of Caphtor (Amos 9:7), the island of Crete, and finally settled in the coastal plain of southwest Canaan known today as the Gaza Strip.

The Philistines had a city-state type government in which the five cities of that coastal plain made up a pentapolis, ruled by five lords. They likely absorbed the Canaanite language, for there never seems to be a language barrier between them and Israel when they communicated. They worshiped Dagon, a grain or fish god. They also were strongly organized militarily, for they at first had the edge over the Israelites because they had weapons made of iron (1 Samuel 13:19–23). The Philistines seemed determined to rule over the Israelites and reduce them to being their slaves (4:9).

The Ark of God had been captured by the Philistines as a trophy of war and taken to Ashdod, one of the cities of the pentapolis. Ashdod was about nineteen miles south of Jerusalem, where the captured Ark was now ensconced in the temple dedicated to Dagon. It was at another temple dedicated to the worship of Dagon in the city of Gaza that Samson had lost his life in an earlier day (Judges 16:23–30). This loss of the Ark of God, then, serves as the backdrop for chapters 5 and 6 in 1 Samuel.

By Our Failing to Promote the Supremacy of God Over All Competing Loyalties – 5:1–12

The Fall of Dagon

The loot the Philistines won at Israel's defeat was the Ark of God. It was placed in the lavish Philistine temple to Dagon at Ashdod, the northern-most city of the Philistine pentapolis, whose other temples to Dagon have been excavated in other cities outside of Philistia at Ebla, Mari, and Ugarit. In some Canaanite legends, Dagon is the father of Baal and thus equivalent to the god El in the Ugaritic/Canaanite pantheon. Generally Dagon is regarded as the god of grain, the one who ensured abundant harvests. He is often depicted as half-fish (upper body), half-man (lower body)—a "*sir*-maid"!

The Philistines set the Ark of the Covenant in their temple, below Dagon's platform, to emphasize the Ark's allegedly inferior and servile position and Dagon's "superior" position. But before the people of Ashdod had finished eating breakfast the next morning, Dagon had fallen face-down on the floor of his temple before the Ark of the Lord. With a delightful sort of irony, v. 3c notes: "They took Dagon and put him back in his place!" Imagine—a god needing a hand from humans! And he had to be put back "in his place"! What kind of god was this anyway? It must have been very "upsetting"!

The Sticking Point of Idolatry

Things got worse: The next morning (5:4), Dagon had again fallen on his face before the Ark of the Lord, but this time, his hands and head broke off; only his body remained intact. Humpty Dumpty had had another great fall. His head and arms lay on the threshold of the temple, and for that reason, so it became a tradition that no one was to step on that spot (v. 5). Imagine the chagrin on the faces of Dagon's worshipers, who came with heavy burdens of their own, only to find that the god they were going to cast all their burdens upon had himself become unglued and was falling to pieces! Perhaps that was a clue to Dagon's worshipers that they should bring some Elmer's Glue to their worship services! It seemed Dagon was getting the "goodness" knocked out of him—if was any there! Surely, though, when your own god cracks up, you must admit to the superiority of the God of gods, the Lord himself. But simply starting a tradition about not stepping on the threshold where Dagon's broken arms and head lay seems rather inadequate! Did not the prophet Zephaniah later warn that God would act against such nonsense in the last days by saying: "On that day, I will punish all who avoid stepping on the threshold, who fill the temple of their gods with violence and deceit"?

In paganism, it's axiomatic that gods need humans to feed and care for them, if not also give transportation. But before we are too quick to criticize such stupid actions, for that is what these actions were, we too must take care of the way we worship the Lord of heaven and earth by singing such ditties as "somehow he needed me." God has no needs! He can rescue his Ark and his own person all by himself! This reason, and no other, is why it is wrongful thinking to imagine we can manipulate God!

Verse 6 says, "The LORD's hand was heavy upon the people of Ashdod and its vicinity." God sent upon them "tumors" or "boils" (not "hemorrhoids," as the NASB suggests), which likely led the citizens to conclude that this plague involved rats and thus could be identified as a bubonic plague. The tumors mentioned here were those that came in the warm and discreet parts of the body. The swellings began as hard tumors, and after a week softened and discharged their contents on the skin, leaving a depression where the hardened lump had been. Death would follow immediately. This seems quite similar to the "Black Death" bubonic plague in Europe (1346–52) and in London (1665–66).

When the men of Ashdod saw this outbreak was clearly linked to the Ark's capture, the Ark suddenly became too hot for them to handle (v. 7). This led the men to seek guidance from the rulers of the Philistines, who advised them to send the Ark on to Gath (v. 8). But the same outbreak from the same plague hit there, young and old (v. 9); they too broke out in tumors. So they sent the Ark on to Ekron, another Philistine city (v. 10).

But Ekron's jaycees met Gath's transportation committee at the city limits, for the people of Ekron cried out that the Ark had been brought to them to kill them (v. 10c). So once again they called on the rulers of the five cities of the Philistines to intervene (v. 11). The Ekronites wanted the Ark sent back to Israel, for once again death had started to fill the city (v. 11c). It was clear by now that the funeral directors of the cities where the Ark had been—Ashdod, Gath and now Ekron—were busier than normal—and not because these cities had more older people than usual, but because of the presence of the Ark of the Covenant. Wherever the Ark went, this disease followed in its wake.

Israel had introduced the Ark into the battlefield thinking they could manipulate its power to help them win the battle, but God will not have his power or person played with as if it were some toy. Nor could the pagan Philistines assume it was only a symbol and that none of God's power was resident within this consecrated part of the furniture of the Tabernacle. Neither will God stand for competing loyalties that take pride of place over his name, reputation and glory. Our Lord will not adapt to being in second place with golf, kids, playing the market, studying for degrees, or any other things like these items being elevated to first place, for they tend to become idols just like Dagon when they are given priority and God is relegated to second place.

By Our Failing to Observe That God Rules Even Over the Most Incidental Affairs of Life – 6:1–12

A Guilt Offering

All the events in chapter 6 took place during the seven months the Ark had been in the Philistine territory (6:1). The lords of the five cities of the Philistines called for their priests and diviners to tell them how they could send the Ark of God back into Israel (v. 2).

The answer of these Philistine priests and diviners was this: "Do not send it away empty" (v. 3a). It must include a "guilt offering" (v. 3b) if they wanted to be healed of the plague. Moreover, if they did send this offering, and healing did come, then they would know that all of this had been as a result of God's hand on them in judgment (v. 3d).

But what kind of guilt offering should they send? This was the new question of the people.

Five Golden Tumors and Five Golden Rats

The answer of the Philistine priests and diviners was this: Send "five golden tumors and five golden rats" (6:4b). These were to be "models of the tumors [from which the people were suffering] and of the rats that are destroying the country" (v. 4d).

God's judgment included a triple threat. His hand was heavy on the Philistines' bodies, gods, and land (v. 5b). The Philistines even showed an awareness of God's work in earlier history, for they warned each other in Philistia not to "harden [their] hearts as the Egyptians and Pharaoh did" (v. 6). This is an important note, for it surely indicates that God meant Israel's history to teach the other nations, while he was acting on behalf of the chosen people. And that word had gotten out to the Gentile nations.

Divine Providence or Chance?

To determine if all of this happened merely as a matter of "chance" (6:9c), or if it was directed by God, Lord of heaven and earth, the Philistines devised an experiment. This specially devised situation would be one that was totally against nature. First, they were to build a new cart, specially designated for the single task of transporting the Ark of God, thereby showing a separation of what was sacred, the Ark, from what was common or ordinary (v. 7a). Then they were to choose "two cows that had [just] calved and [had] never been yoked" to a cart before (v. 7b). The cows were to be hitched to the cart, but their newly born calves were to be taken from them and left behind penned up (v. 7c). This experiment would run counter to all of nature, for these cows ordinarily would not leave their calves behind, and it would not be easy for them to pull a cart they if had never done so previously. Those who were raised on a farm can attest to the veracity of this experiment; if any have tried to take a cow out to pasture with the calf still in the barn—it is an impossible task. (I know—I myself tried when I was ten years old.)

The Philistines loaded the "chest containing the gold rats and the tumors" (v. 11) on the cart. To their surprise, the cows took off immediately for the Israelite city of Beth-Shemesh, "keeping on the road [but] lowing all the way" (v. 12). In this manner, the cows showed they wanted instead to be with their calves, but God was using their "lowing" to speak to the Philistines in a "low" voice. When people cannot and will not listen to the plain teaching of the God's Word, he will speak to them through cows rather than through the words of the prophets. God was meeting the Philistines on their own grounds. As the plague was withdrawn as suddenly as it had appeared, some may have slapped "I Survived the Plague of 1070" or "Glad That's Over With" bumper-stickers onto their chariots! But God was using pain for those who had become tone-deaf to the preaching of his Word through his messengers. Remember, they were dealing with the Savior of the whole world.

It is clear that God can speak even through the small events of life such as two cows that go with the Ark straight back to where it came from, even when everything in their natures beckoned them to stay with their calves. This was not chance or luck; it was God's sovereign, providential work on behalf of a people who little deserved his grace and mercy.

By Our Failing to Respect the Holiness of God in Our Worship of Him – 6:13–7:1

More on Beth-Shemesh

Beth-Shemesh was indeed a Levitical city (Joshua 21:16; 1 Chronicles 6:59; Judges 1:35). It was only a small town. The mound on which it stood is on a ridge between two valleys that meet in the west. In the two valleys, wheat could be grown. Thus, the cow-drawn cart came upon the harvesters probably during the wheat-harvest time of May/June (v. 13). We do not know who this "Joshua" was, or where his field was (v. 14), but when the reapers looked up and saw the Ark of God was on this cart that was not being led by any individuals, the people all stopped their work and used the "large rock" (v. 14b) alongside of where the cart stopped as the rock on which they would offer sacrifices to God (v. 14c). The rock served as a table on which to put the Ark and the Philistines' offerings, and it served also as a natural altar to give thanks to God (v. 15). All of this was observed by the five rulers of the Philistines who had followed as unobserved as possible and then returned home to Philistia that day (v. 16). Just imagine what they told the people of their five cities about the God of Israel and what had taken place with the cows and their calves!

It is true that unblemished male animals were normally required for burnt offerings in Israel (Lev 1:3; 22:19, yet God apparently accepted the sacrifice of these two female cows, for they could not be used for any other purpose since they had borne the holy Ark of God.

More Evidence of Disregard for God's Word – 6:19–7:1

In a reckless move, the citizens of Beth-Shemesh "looked into" or "gawked at" at the holy Ark of God in the field of Joshua, and as a result, seventy of them died (v. 19). Even though Beth-Shemesh was a Levitical town with Levites, they did not cover the Ark as prescribed by the Law of God (Numbers 4:5, 19–20). Perhaps this was but another evidence of the prolonged disregard for the Word of God as much as just plain carelessness as well.

To better grasp the severity of God's judgment against the seventy, the verb translated "looked into" can also carry the force of "inspected the insides," "gawked at it" or even "touched it."

The Hebrew text actually said "He smote the people, fifty thousand and three score and ten men," but this seems a later textual corruption, for the town of Beth-Shemesh was indeed small. Why the whole town was affected is not clear unless the interpretation given by the Jewish historian Josephus is correct. He claimed that those who touched the Ark were not worthy to touch it as the priests were, so judgment fell on all.

The question that was left standing was this: "Who can stand in the presence of the LORD, this holy God?" (v. 20) Was the death that came on the seventy a result of the disease that had spread from the Philistine contacts with the rats? Regardless of what it was, it certainly did strike awe and deep respect for the holiness and separateness of God from all that was common and ordinary. God's sanctity is violated when we show indifference to his person, presence and holiness. That sanctity is also violated when we express apathy or treat that which is holy with mere curiosity and commonality. But God will vindicate his own honor and holiness in the midst of his people. Curiously, the people blamed God and not themselves.

The answer as to who may stand in the presence of such a holy God is answered for example in Psalm 15:1–2. It reads:

> Lord, who may dwell in your sanctuary?
> Who may live in your holy hill?
> He who walks blamelessly
> And does what is righteous,
> Who speaks the truth from his heart…

Malachi 3:2 also asks the same question:

> But who can endure the day of his coming?
> Who can stand when he appears?

God must be respected and approached reverently. Worship must be radically theocentric, for it cannot take its rise from human emotions alone. Instead, it must begin with God's majesty, magnificence and sovereignty. There are human formats of worship that are inimical to God, and those must be carefully screened off from use when we approach him.

Those left around Beth-Shemesh sent to the people of Kiriath Jearim (v. 21) to come and take it to their town instead of where the Ark landed. So these men came and took it to Abinadab's house (7:1). We are not told that Abinadab or his son Eleazar were priests, but the name Eleazar is linked with some priestly lines (Exodus 6:23). This family continued to care for the Ark for some twenty years until King David came and took it to Jerusalem.

Conclusions

1. The power that is found in sacred items such as the Ark of the Covenant may not be manipulated for our own uses even though the power is still present in the sacred item itself.

2. The power and authority of God can be seen in its direct confrontation with the pagan idols of that day.

3. God's holiness is not to be toyed with as if we can play with it to our own amusement, for it will turn deadly against us for us disregard when we could and should have known better.

4. The absence of godly fear indicates an absence of the knowledge of God.

Lesson 5

It's Time to Serve the Lord Only

1 Samuel 7:2–17

The town where the tabernacle had stood, Shiloh, was sacked by the Philistines around 1050 B.C.E. Eli, the overweight priest, also had fallen off his chair and died on hearing of the capture of the Ark of God and the loss of his sons Hophni and Phinehas. Following these events, apparently Samuel felt compelled to return home to Ramah, which he had left as a child when he was around three years old, as his mother Hannah brought him as she had promised to serve in the house of the Lord.

The village of Ramah had seen a lot of changes in the twenty years since Samuel's birth (7:2), but it was here that he would marry, raise his children (whose names were Joel, meaning "Yahweh is God" and Abiah, meaning "Yahweh is my father"), and it was there he spent the rest of his life.

Samuel carried out his priestly functions from Ramah as he visited Bethel, Gilgal and Mizpah on a regular circuit. However, he was never invited to resume the priestly functions at Nob, where the Tabernacle was now located, even though it was only a few miles from his home. Instead, Samuel served as a judge (7:6, 15, 17) and officiated as a priest at Ramah, Bethel, Mizpah and at times at Gilgal, apparently without the approval of Eli's descendants.

Despite what seemed a deliberate shunning of this prophet and man of God, Samuel served without rancor or bitterness as he single-handedly set himself to the task of rebuilding Israel's ruined state. Never did he turn back from his calling from God (ch. 3); he served faithfully all his days during this period that was largely passed over in silence and represented one of the dark pages in Israel's history, from both a political and religious standpoint. The Israelites remained as vassals to the Philistines all during this period, and the people sank deep into idolatry

(7:3–4). But it is hard to imagine that it was also during these same twenty years of subservience to the Philistines, and the people's awful commitment to the foreign gods of Ashtaroth and Baal, that Samuel needed to be active, for the people needed to hear God's Word more than ever. I think that is what he did all those years: preach the word of God.

But a day came when, in God's providence, Samuel summoned all Israel to turn back to the Lord by calling for national repentance (vv. 3–4). It is amazing that the people recognized his authority and flocked to hear what he had to say, for already the evil they had done had wracked up a heap of trouble for them. Though he is not mentioned in chapters 4–6, Samuel had indeed continued to serve the Lord all during those twenty years. The events of those days seemed to focus instead on the Ark of God. But Samuel remained faithful, for when the right moment came to call Israel to repentance, the people seemed more than ready to hear what he had to say. During those bitter years of enemy occupation of the land, the people shed many tears. They were pressed into seeking after the Lord by the very impossibility of the situation they had brought on themselves by their sin.

We Must Commit Ourselves to the Lord Alone – 7:2–4

Twenty Long Years of Suffering

All during the long, dark period of those twenty years, while the Ark of the Covenant remained in Kiriath Jearim, Samuel must have continued to teach the Word of God to the people. This could be seen in the fact that because of the persistent teaching of God's Word, the spiritual sensitivities of the people were moved from a deep mourning over the state of affairs they found themselves in, to some new seeds of spiritual hunger (7:2).

This may have been about the time when Samson died as he brought down the Philistine temple on himself and some 3000 Philistines—all of whom were killed by this collapse. That event may have jolted the nation out of its sorrowful complacency into a willingness to renounce their idolatry and a desire to commit their lives to the Lord as they renewed their commitment to God's covenant with them. Samuel also believed it was time for the nation to return to the Lord, their One and only True Sovereign.

A Call to Return to the Lord

In verses 2–3, "all the people of Israel lamented after the LORD," and "the whole house of Israel" was called to return to him. This meant that all Israel had heard the word of the Lord, apparently from the prophet Samuel's own mouth, and that by the close of the second decade of their subservience to Philistia, the people saw how sad and destitute their lives were when they were deprived of God's love and grace. The idols of the land could not fulfill the hunger of their souls. It was high time Israel repented of their sin.

Samuel called on the people to renounce their false gods and the hardened condition of their hearts. If they were to come back to the Lord, as all indications seemed to point to, then it had to be with: (1) a full heart dedication to turn to God, (2) a ridding of themselves of false gods like Baal and Ashtoreth, (3) a choice to commit themselves to the Lord, and (4) a true desire to serve him alone (v. 3). The command to put away their gods was the same one that had been given years earlier when revival came to Jacob and his family (Genesis 35:2). A whole-hearted fellowship with the Living God with competing loyalties to other gods was totally out of line with any claim to worshiping God. Then the people were to fix their hearts in God. This was the reverse of wavering states of mind, which went from sighing and lamenting their sad national or personal state of affairs to coming by occasionally to consult God. But if they really were serious, they had to empty their lives of all service to false gods and instead fill their lives with glad service to the Lord alone. Then God would deliver them out of the hands of the Philistines when they turned in true confession and repentance.

These were the basic steps for the renewal and revival of any people anywhere on the face of the earth. There had to be steps in forsaking of all their sin, no matter how much of that sin they had enjoyed. There had to be a giving of their whole heart and life over to the Lord as the only Lord of their life. And there had to be a commitment of one's way of life to serve the Lord from that time forward without reservation or any competition.

Recall 1 Samuel 3:19: "None of his [God's] words fell to the ground." Thus the people's sense of being forsaken, and their sighing and crying, which had increased because of their oppressors' incursions on their land and possessions, and because of the powerful ministry of God's Word through the prophet Samuel—all of this was used by God to prepare Israel for a revival.

This penitential return to God from idolatry and abandoning their loyalty to him was closely connected in the Hebrew text with five clauses. There is no gap between them in vv. 2–3. The Hebrew literally read, "And it came to pass," "and the days multiplied," "and they grew to 20 years," "and all the house of Israel mourned," "and Samuel said." Thus, the condition of the people during these twenty years was stressed by this extended series of clauses all grammatically joined almost like a list of what was happening to prepare them for revival. The Philistines had been the overlords of Israel for forty years, but in these last twenty years, it had become unbearable.

We Must Confess Our Sins and Pray to the Lord – 7: 5–9

Revival Time at Mizpah

Samuel called for a day of confession and fasting at Mizpah (v. 5; the name means "watch tower"), one of the cities on Samuel's regular circuit (v. 15). It is amazing that Samuel seems to have been such a recognized authority that the people quickly gathered in response to his order to assemble. They had few if any other options; they were in desperate straits. Apparently, they began to realize what the Word of God had taught through Samuel was real and they were in deep need of God's cleansing if they were to find any relief.

Mizpah is likely a mountain site (2935 feet), some five miles northwest of Jerusalem in the tribal territory of Benjamin, known also today as Nebi Samwil. It had a breathtaking view; from there one could see the coastline of the Mediterranean Sea to the west, Jerusalem and the Mount of Olives to the southeast, the Jordan Valley farther to the southeast, and Mount Gerizim to the north as well as the promontory of Mount Carmel to the northwest. Some say Mizpah is associated with modern Tell en-Nasbeh, also in Benjamite territory, but most favor Nebi Samwil as the correct identification as the site.

Four Happenings That Resulted

When the conditions are right, revival is inevitable, as it also was on this day in Israel's history. Just as rain must fall when the atmospheric conditions are ripe, so revival must come when God's people meet the conditions for a revival. All the elements for a revival were now in place (see vv. 3–4); it would now seem to be impossible for God *not* to visit them with a revival.

The first event that took place was contrition for their sin (v. 6). After the people had assembled at Mizpah, Samuel began to "intercede" on their behalf (v. 5b). "They drew water and poured it out before the LORD" (v. 6). This act was a symbol of the people's hearts that were now poured out towards the Lord. It was a sign of deep contrition and humiliation for their sin, which was now all the misery and distress their sin had caused them, which they regarded as water spilt on the ground and could not be gathered together again. This same figure of speech is used in Lamentations 2:19 and Psalm 22:15.

Second, they "fasted" on that day (v. 6b) as they expressed repentance by doing without food, afflicting their bodies to join in their souls' grief.

Third, they "confessed" to God their sin by saying, "We have sinned against the LORD" (v. 6c). In revivals, confession of sin must be as public in the act of confession as the sin was public in its enactment. But if the sin was not public, there was no sense in dragging all that dirty linen out in public as a spectacle, for it tended only to sensationalize the sinner and not his Lord.

Fourth, in v. 6d Samuel's work was that of "judge" of the people's sin. He did this by directing and ordering the people as they required in some cases, for example, to make restitution for stolen property and the like, so the confession of sin was shown to be accompanied with action.

Note again v. 5: Samuel, in his role as prophet, promised to pray for the people. Thus, the highest purpose of this (as for any) "Man of God" and his calling was to pray for those he served. He would present the people as objects of God's grace and mercy. In this case, he would present them as those God would forgive for their sin and for the blotting out of their iniquity. To pray in this way was to put the people in a right relationship with God and to prepare the way for their deliverance from the Philistine oppression.

The Enemy Responds

Whenever there is a spiritual stirring on earth and the hearts of the people become repentant, often Satan responds with an immediate attack. In this case, when the Philistines heard that all Israel had assembled at Mizpah (v. 7), they saw this event as a political revolt against them. In a way, they were correct, for revival always brings with it a *freedom* that one has not had in the past. This is why teachers and ministers should pray for those to whom they teach and preach, that God would make the teaching effective and protect those who respond from the snares of the devil, who loathes to see those he had previously bound in sin being set free of his devices.

That is why the people significantly and importantly called out to Samuel, "Do not stop crying out to the LORD our God for us, that he may rescue us from the hand of the Philistines" (v. 8). Now that they had been restored to fellowship with God, they begged for his intervention on their behalf.

Samuel's Prayer and Sacrifice

Samuel presented the people in a twofold priestly function: in prayer for them, and by offering up a suckling lamb as a whole-burnt offering to God for them (v. 9a). This lamb was about seven days old (Leviticus 22:27), and it was wholly or totally given up to the Lord, indicating a total dedication of all that Israel was, or could be, to God. As a result, the Lord answered Samuel and his prayer on behalf of Israel (v. 9b).

We Must Count On God's Help and Act Boldly – 7:10–17

A Thunder Storm

Even while Samuel was in the midst of offering this sacrifice to the Lord, the Philistines drew near to engage in battle with Israel (v. 10). Whereas at other times God sent down fire in answer to prayer to him (e.g., 1 Kings 18), in this instance he "thundered with a loud thunder against the Philistines" (v. 10b). The thunder threw the Philistines "into a panic" and they were routed by the Israelites (v. 10c). The men of Israel, when they saw the panic that had overtaken the Philistines, rushed out of Mizpah and slaughtered a large number of the enemy all the way up to "Beth-car" (v. 11b), a site that has not yet been identified.

This was not the first time that weather had played a part in the outcome of a battle (Joshua 10:11; Judges 5:4, 20, 21; 1 Sam 2:10). Josephus claimed the thunder and lightning in this case had also been accompanied by an earthquake, but whatever it was, it was enough to unnerve the otherwise battle-tested Philistines. It may also be a factor that the sudden violent storm confused these Baal worshipers, who called him the god of the storm. So why had their god turned against them? What was going wrong?

A Memorial Stone – "Ebenezer"

Such an important deliverance from the hand of God was not to be left unnoticed and forgotten, for Samuel saw to it that a war-memorial was set up in this prominent place to help future generations remember what God had done for Israel there. This memorial did not list the names of the dead; it was for the praise and honor of the Living God who had won the victory for them. This stone would be called "Ebenezer," meaning "stone of help" or "stone of the Helper" (v. 12a). God had been elsewhere referred to by that same name, Ezer, e.g. Psalm 115:9–11: "He [God] is their help and shield." Samuel explained this "stone's" name: "Thus far [i.e., all the way and up to this point] the LORD has helped us" (12b), meaning God's help had extended to Mizpah, where the battle had begun, and had continued all the way up to "Shen" ("the tooth," referencing the tooth-like crag called Jeshanah; see 2 Chronicles 13:19). It could also have been not just a geographical reference to these two cities but also a spiritual and temporal reference, such as: "Until now," and all these past days and events, and up to this point also, God has helped us! But the finality of this event was clear: "the Philistines were subdued and [they] did not invade Israelite territory again" (v. 13) for some time.

Some point to a possible problem with the name "Ebenezer," because in 4:1b is an earlier site with the same name. But this may have been an intentional duplication: The first reference indicated one of the original battles with the Philistines, where they defeated the Israelites; the one in 7:12 now refers to a battle that ended in a marvelous victory and the expulsion of the Philistines from Israel for a long time. Thus the two events use the same place name and are thus related, but the outcomes are vastly different.

The Rest of Samuel's Lifetime

Samuel's greatness can be seen in vv. 15–17; he served as a judge, or more accurately a governor, over much of Israel as they came to him at the sites of Mizpah, Bethel and Gilgal, where he made his periodic circuit to each of these centers (v. 16). Samuel also established schools (or should we say "seminaries") for the younger prophets (called the "sons of the prophets"), in Ramah, Bethel, Gilgal and Mizpah. Presumably these prophets were sent out throughout the whole land of Israel to minister the Word of God. Samuel's name stands out as a symbol of that which was pure and upright, for his silent hand of influence had the effect of steadying the state of the country.

Samuel, the "Man of God" (an early title used for a prophet, see 9:6–10; just as Elisha is so designated in 2 Kings 5:8, 14–15), was more commonly known in those days not primarily as a "prophet" but a "seer," for that was the older name for this prophetic institution (9:9b), in which these "seers" could see the future or find things that had been lost. In fact, Samuel even claimed the title when Saul and his servants accosted him in (9:19) about where their lost donkeys could be found. He acknowledged, "I am the seer." But there can be little doubt that much of the prophetic movement in the Old Testament owes a huge debt of gratitude to Samuel for the way he exemplified what Moses foresaw as the institution of the prophets.

Conclusions

1. To serve God alone is to declare him as one's only Sovereign with no rivals at all.

2. If we forsake the Lord, since he is a holy and jealous God, he will chase us with his love and mercy, allowing disaster to fall on us if he must, to bring us to our senses and get our attention to receive his love.

3. Our prayer should be like the hymn puts it: "Send a great revival in my heart; let the Holy Spirit come and take control; Oh, send a great revival in my heart!"

4. When we fix our hearts and prayers on him and confess our sin in true repentance to him, he is more than willing to forgive us and to bring new life in Yeshua.

Lesson 6

Israel's Demand to Have a King Just Like Other Nations

1 Samuel 8:1–22

Samuel, the "Seer," was declining in years and apparently also in popularity. A new generation had arisen, one that had only heard from their parents how the Lord had spectacularly delivered them from their enemies, the Philistines, throughout the former years, but such actual deliverances this younger generation had not personally seen for themselves. In fact, the most-recent great defeat of Israel's nemesis was the expulsion of the Philistines some twenty-five years ago. During those same twenty-five years, "the hand of the LORD was against the Philistines" (7:13). Thus, as long as Samuel was judging the twelve tribes of Israel, their enemies were unable to prevail against them, for God's eye was upon Israel to keep them, and he used Samuel to intercede in prayer for the nation as a means of keeping them safe!

But now that Samuel was about sixty-five years old, in the eyes of this new generation he was just plain too old to continue as the nation's leader (12:2), even though Samuel's actual death is not recorded in Scripture until later (25:1). The younger generation was concerned about Samuel's age, and they did not think his two sons were spiritually suited to lead the nation as their father had. Furthermore, Samuel had already "appointed" his two sons—his firstborn, Joel (whose name means "the LORD is God"), and Abijah (whose name means "my [divine] father is the LORD"; 8:2)—to serve as "judges" at the sanctuary in Beersheba, a town near the far southern border of the Israelite territory—some 57 miles south of Samuel's hometown of Ramah. However, the sons did not walk in the ways of their father Samuel; they "turned aside after dishonest gain and accepted bribes and perverted justice" (8:3). Joel and Abijah were, of course, entitled to a portion of the sacrifices the people of Beersheba brought to the sanctuary there, but apparently they felt that was not enough, so they indulged in accepting bribes, a fixing of the charges for a fee, and reversing the court charges for others for a fee! In some ways they were much like Eli's sons, but Samuel's sons at least did not seem to indulge in sexual sins as had Eli's sons.

These circumstances seemed to give three solid reasons why a call went up from the land for a king in Israel to match what the other nations had as leaders. Never mind that the Lord God was Israel's king and that he was the One who had given stability to the land and leadership for all those years. The three reasons the elders and populace gave for a change in Samuel's leadership were: (1) he was now too old for his job as judge, (2) his two sons did not walk in the way of the Lord as he did, and (3) it was time to bring their administration up-to-date with an actual king that matched what the other nations practiced and possessed.

An Ambivalent Attitude Towards Israel's Future Kingship

Scholars over the years have claimed to have found in 1 Samuel 8–12 a series of individual story units—some pro-monarchical (favoring a king) and others anti-monarchical (Israel maintaining her own leaders instead of being under God's rule).[1] This division allegedly represents different attitudes and responses to the idea of having a monarchy and kingship in Israel. Generally the anti-monarchical units were identified as being 1 Samuel 8:1, 21; 10:17–27 and 12:1–25, while those units that allegedly favored a pro-monarchical stance were said to be in 1 Samuel 9:1–10:16 and 11:1–15. But if this analysis is correct, it leaves a dilemma: How could Scripture at once both seem to approve and disapprove the concept of a monarchy? It would be self-contradictory— which didn't bother critical scholars but did bother conservative scholars who trusted the integrity of the Scriptures.

The answer to this problem is seen in the fact that this same ambivalence is also present even within the units that have been labeled

---

1. See the discussion of issues related to these problems in Walter C. Kaiser, Jr., et. al., *Hard Sayings of the Bible* (Downers Grove, IL: InterVarsity Press, 1996), 202–203.

to one side or the other. We must ask, therefore, what is the cause of this love-hate attitude toward Israel having a king like the other nations? Why this ambivalence?

As Robert Vannoy shows, the covenantal relationship (expressed in 1 Samuel 11:14–12:25) best explains this ambivalence from within the text itself.[2] Thus the most-important point is not the fact of the *presence* of a king in Israel; it is instead the *kind* of kingship and the *reasons* for wanting a monarchy in the first place. It was a denial that the Lord was their king and their leader as much as it was a turn-down and a rejection also of Samuel.

There is no question that the *presence* of a king in Israel was fully compatible and very much part of God's earlier plan and covenant that someday Israel would have a king. But what hurt the Lord and Samuel the most was the people's improper *motive* for asking for a king in the first place: They wanted to "be like the other nations" (8:20) and have a king to lead them when they went out to fight their battles! This demand was tantamount to breaking the covenant and rejecting God as their sovereign Lord (8:7, 10:19). They were deliberately forgetting how God had provided for them in the past. Had he not protected them and gone before them in battle many a time so far? If so, why was Samuel's old age such an important factor that it would demand a whole new administration model? Had not God delivered the nation time after time up to that point? What was all the rush to change what had been working so well in the past?

The concept of a monarchy was fully within God's plan, even as far back as the days of Abraham (Genesis 17:6, 16). This cannot be over-emphasized! Far distant in time, there had been in the blessing of Jacob a hint of the establishment of a continuing dynasty in Israel (Gen. 49:10). In fact, Israel was called to be "a kingdom of priests and a holy nation" (Exodus 19:6). The non-Israelite prophet Balaam, who had been hired by King Balak of Moab to curse Israel and put a jinx on them, had also referred to a monarchical rule in Israel in his fourth prophecy (Numbers 24:17–19). Likewise, Moses also had

---

2. Robert Vannoy, *Covenant Renewal at Gilgal* (Cherry Hill, NJ: Mack Publishing, 1970), 228.

outlined the expectation for future kings in Israel (Deuteronomy 17:14–20). Finally, God himself is recognized as "King" in Israel (Num. 23:21; Deut. 33:5). Any king who was crowned as leader in Israel had to understand from the start that he was to rule *under* God's sovereign oversight and dominion!

Five Serious Problems with the Secular Form of Kingship

1 Samuel 8:11–18 lists five huge problems with all contemporary and secular forms of kingship known in the ancient Near East of those days. These issues were not hypothetical; archaeological documents excavated at the sites of Alalakh and Ugarit, from roughly the same time as Samuel's, show the identical issues he raised.[3] Samuel warned Israel, as a word from God, that the problems they would face were the following:

1. A military draft of Israelites,
2. The servitude of the populace,
3. Widespread confiscation of private property by the king,
4. Taxation of the people, and
5. Loss of personal liberty!

This straightforward delineation of "the manner/ways of the [secular] king" (Hebrew *mishpat hammelek*, 8:9) served to define the function of the pagan kings in the ancient Near East. Up to this point in Israel, each family had been autonomous and under the leadership of the elders of that community. They had been beholden to no one else. But now that a king would have the authority to demand military and agricultural conscription, it would severely cut Israel's liberties and rule from under the feet of the elders.

Not even the women in Israelite families would escape domination if Israel adopted a king; the women of those households could be conscripted as "perfumers, cooks, and bakers" to serve the royal household! Moreover, taxation would become increasingly oppressive to

---

3. I. Mendelsohn, "Samuel's Denunciation of Kingship in Light of Akkadian Documents from Ugarit," *Bulletin of the American Schools of Oriental Research* No. 143 (Oct. 1956): 17.

the point where the people were made virtual slaves, and they would one day cry out for liberation.

The Nation Rejects Samuel's Warnings and Cried for a King

Samuel had tried his best to warn the people that what they were asking for would hurt them badly (8:10–18). That king would take a tenth of their grain and vintage (v. 14) and give it to his attendants. He would also take a tenth of their flocks, and the people would become "slaves" to the new king (v. 17). The king would have the right to take the peoples' menservants and maidservants as well as the best of their cattle and donkeys for his own personal use (v. 16). Samuel foresaw a coming day when the people would cry out for relief from the king they had chosen, but the Lord would not answer in that day, for the people had demanded they have a king (v. 18).

Despite such warnings, the people remained obstinate. They wanted what they wanted! Their hearts were set on having a mortal king, and that was that! Without knowing what they were doing, they were courting the despotism of an intolerable yoke for the future generations—a yoke they would not be able to break (v. 18). What had begun as a mere *request* (8:5) was made a *demand* (v. 19). The elders and people were unresponsive to any clear reasons, or to any of the prophet Samuel's wisdom to the contrary. Instead of waiting for God's appointed time when he would fulfill their desire for a king in a better way, they insisted that former form of theocracy they had been under must be rejected and they be given a king immediately.

Ingratitude is hard to bear, if you are the object of its insult, but the Lord instructed Samuel, "Listen to/obey them and give them a king" (v. 21). So let us look more closely at the passage as we turn from these apologetical issues to the abiding message for our day.

Replace God's Rule with the Rule of a King – 8:5–8, 19–20

The elders of the land confronted Samuel with the fact that he was growing old, just as Eli, Samuel's predecessor as priest and judge, had grown old before him (2:22). Moreover, these elders wanted nothing to do with dynastic succession that would include Samuel's two sons, who clearly did not walk with the Lord. As a result, the elders were now calling for a king just like the other nations had (8:5). Since Samuel's sons were downright scoundrels, the elder's solution was to replace both the Lord and Samuel as leaders of the nation with a human king who would physically lead the nation into battle. This later point seemed to be the real hidden agenda behind their request: a king who would boldly "go out before us and fight our battles" (v. 20). Perhaps it was the real hostile pressure that was coming from the Philistines to the west, and a bit of the Ammonite pressure from the east, that played a part in prompting the monarchical question (8:20, 9:16, 10:1). The elders longed for a permanent military leader who would build up a standing army that could withstand any invasion, and one who would lead them into battle! In their view, it was time for an immediate change!

As discussed above, the demand for a king was not wrong in itself; in days long before Samuel, Moses had shown such a change would one day be in altogether in keeping with Deuteronomy 17:14–20. So, the fault of the elders and people in Samuel's day was in their *motive* for asking for a king, not in the request itself. But where were the prayers of the elders and the people crying out instead to God for his solution to their problems and his deliverance as he had acted in their former days? Instead, the nation was now rejecting the Lord who had brought them out of Egypt and had ever since delivered them time after time. Now the nation no longer wanted to claim their help from the Lord; they wanted a new form of government to lead them. It was an outright rejection of the Lord and his servant Samuel.

Replace "God's Ways" with the "King's Ways" – 8:11–18, 21–22

The Lord told Samuel, "Now Listen to them; however, warn them solemnly and let them know what the king who will reign over you will do" (8:9). Samuel traced for the people the abuses of the "king's way" (vv. 11–18).

Four times Samuel used the verb "to take" (Hebrew *laqah*; 8:11,13, 14, 16) to indicate that it was this king that they demanded who would take away from them all the stuff they had thought was theirs. Thus, the king would "take" Israel's sons in the draft to serve as his charioteers and horsemen; others he would take for farm labor; still others to produce weapons. Their daughters were also subject to the draft, for they would serve as perfume-makers, cooks and bakers for the palace. Likewise, this new king would "take" their fields, vineyards and crops. The tax burden would become increasingly heavy.

Despite all these warnings, the people refused to heed them. Their minds were already made up. Yet God had promised that none of Samuel's words would fall to the ground (3:19). Israel would not (and did not) recognize the prophet's wisdom; they simply did not listen to God's voice through his servant; they just plain refused to heed any warnings! (8:19, 22)

Replace "Being Holy" to the Lord with Being "Like the Other Nations" – 8:5, 19–20

Ever since we were children, most of us disliked being different and distinct from everyone else; we would rather blend in with the crowd. Perhaps this was another reason why the elders and the people wanted to have a king "like all the nations." No matter how severely Samuel warned them of the loss of their personal freedoms and possessions the nation as they surrendered them to their sought-after king, their minds had been made up long ago. They likely chanted and marched in favor of a monarchical government, saying: "No [prophet or God will rule over us], but a king must be over us, and we—we too—shall be like all the nations" (8:19b–20a). Once Israel had a king, the nation felt they would fit in with the rest of the nations.

What Israel had forgotten was that from the beginning of the peoples' existence, they had been set aside by God to be distinctive and different people of his possession! In Deuteronomy 4:32–40, the Lord taught this very same truth through a series of questions. For example, had any nation ever heard God speaking to it directly from heaven as Israel had at Mount Sinai? Had God ever taken a nation like Israel out of the bondage and subjugation of another powerful nation like Egypt in such a dramatic and convincing way? Of course, Israel was different, but look at the reason why.

Israel was a nation that been called to be different, or as the Scripture put it, "to be holy" (Leviticus 18:2). Instead of the peoples' wish to stay in step with the culture, they were to pay no attention to this crooked and perverse generation! Their whole lifestyle was to be one of purity; their lives were to be marked with seeking justice for those who could not help themselves; they were to practice chastity and faithfulness in their marriages; and they were to rejoice in the God who had loved them and promised to bless them so richly.

Conclusions

1. All too often we mortals tend to dictate to God the form our help should take, rather than looking to God for his solutions and guidance.

2. At times, our Lord will yield to our requests even though he knows what is better for us (8:7a, 9). He gives what we think we want and then he sends leanness to our souls instead, which is given to remind us that his ways are best (Psalm 106:15).

3. To ask our Lord for a substitute means of governing our lives is to state an outright rejection of his rule and reign over us.

4. Too often we think that the answer to our problems is found in one or more of our techniques or some other mechanical or reasoned mortal approach; however, all this time the Lord had the perfect solution for us and the problem we faced.

Lesson 7

Finding Lost Donkeys
and Anointing Saul as King

1 Samuel 9:1–10:16

Chapter 9 began by describing a particular man from the tribe of Benjamin, named Saul, son of Kish. He seemed to be a wealthy farmer, or at least he was called "a man of standing" in the community. Saul himself was said to be "an impressive young man … a head taller than any of the others … [and] … without equals among the Israelites" (9:1–2). That was high praise, to say the least. The Lord wanted Saul's pedigree placed ahead of finishing the story about Saul and his servant searching for his father's lost donkeys.

The Miraculous Signs That Signaled the Hand of God – 9:3–27

It is most interesting that the Lord used the incident of the lost donkeys to bring Samuel into contact with Saul! In a way, the appearance of the donkeys sort of framed this whole story of the anointing of Saul (vv. 3, 10, 16). Ronald Youngblood describes the irony of this situation: Just as Saul was sent to look for the donkeys, which were not immediately found (9:3–4, 20; 10:2, 14, 16), so the people were intent on searching for a king and found Saul, a bashful and reluctant candidate, who also could not be immediately found when the time came, for he was hiding among the baggage (10:21–22).[1]

Despite all the unknowns in this section as to what was going on, note how often the verb *matsa'*, "to find," occurs: Twice in 9:4, Saul and his servant could not "find" the donkeys. Twice in v. 8, the servant "found" the prophet's fee. In v. 11, Saul and his servant "found" girls going to draw water; twice in v. 13 they told Saul and his servant to

---

1. Ronald J. Youngblood, "1 and 2 Samuel," in *The Expositor's Bible Commentary*, eds. Tremper Longman & David E. Garland (Grand Rapids, MI: Zondervan, 2009), 99.

hasten to "find" (meet) the "seer." In v. 20, Samuel assured Saul the donkeys had been "found"; he restated it in 10:3 when the men "found" (met) him near Rachel's tomb. In 10:7, Saul was told God's power would come over him as he would "find" occasion to defeat Israel's enemies. In v. 14, Saul told his uncle the donkeys had not been "found"; in v. 16, his uncle assured him they were "found" (10:16). It was in this way that a kingdom was introduced to the people! What a "find"!

In their search for these straying donkeys, that by that time had been declared to be totally lost, Saul and his servant searched the borderlands between the tribes of Benjamin and Ephraim, but with no results (9:4). The locations of Shaalim and Shalisha, through which the two of them passed, are unknown, but these names may have been singled out as geographical markers because of their similar-sounding names to that of Saul.

By now Saul felt they should return home, for perhaps his father would by now be more worried about them than about the donkeys. His servant, however, observed that they were near the place where the "man of God" (another name for a "prophet" or "seer"; v. 9b), lived, which no doubt was the town of Ramah (v. 14).

When Saul reminded his servant if they were going to inquire of the "man of God," they had no gift they to give the prophet for his help, for such a courtesy was usually expected (Amos 7:12). Surprisingly, the servant said he had a "quarter of a shekel of silver." Coinage was not invented in the ancient Near East until the seventh century B.C.E., but apparently this was a much earlier example of pieces of silver being used for trade.

Saul and his servant "went up the hill" to where they were told the seer had indeed come to that town (9:11), likely his hometown of Ramah, which accordingly meant "height." When they came to the top of the hill and asked if the "seer" was there, they were told he had just arrived and was now ready to participate in the sacrificial ritual at the "high place" (Hebrew *bamah*, v. 12). There was at that place an open-air sanctuary, which usually was located on the highest spot in the town. The two men were urged to hurry to meet the man of God there (vv. 12–

13). The men arrived just as Samuel, who was on his way to officiate at the sacrifice, was proceeding to do so (v. 14).

The day before Saul arrived in Ramah, the Lord had told Samuel that at about that same time on the morrow, he would send to him a man from the land of Benjamin, whom he, Samuel, was to "anoint' as "leader" over the people of Israel (vv. 15–16). The verb to "anoint" comes from the Hebrew *mashiah*, "anointed [one], Messiah." Samuel was to anoint Saul as "leader" (*nagid*). He used this term rather than *melek*, meaning "king." *Nagid*, "leader," is "[one] who is placed in front," or "[one' who is given prominence." This may also have functioned as a title for the "king-designate" or as "king-elect."

The task this newly appointed leader was to have is described in this manner: He was to deliver God's people from the power of the Philistines (10:16b). Moreover, God said to Samuel that he had looked on the people of Israel and he had heard their outcry! (v. 16c)

Sure enough, as soon as Samuel caught sight of Saul, the Lord confirmed what had simultaneously sprung into his mind: "This is the man I spoke to you about; he will govern my people [Israel]" (v. 17). Saul came up to Samuel and asked where he might find the seer's house (v. 18); Samuel replied, "I am the seer." Samuel instructed Saul to go ahead of him to the "high place" (*bamah*), for he was going to eat with the prophet Samuel that very day and then Samuel would send him on his way to his father. In addition, Samuel would tell Saul all that was in his heart. Also, Saul was not to worry about the donkeys, which his father had lost three days ago; they had since been found. But for now, Saul was the one who was the "desire" of all Israel (v. 20). The word "desire" would appear later as a Messianic term for those in the Davidic line (Haggai 2:7).

Saul humbly declined all the praise Samuel heaped on him and his family. He protested that he was only a Benjamite, which was the smallest tribe in Israel and, even at that, his clan was the least significant of his whole tribe (v. 21).

Samuel then brought Saul into a "hall" and seated him at the head of the table (v. 22). The Hebrew word for "hall," *lishka*, usually denotes a room found in a temple or sanctuary. Often such rooms were used as apartments for those who ministered at the sanctuary, or were just used for storerooms of the tithe brought to the house of God. In the case of the "hall" at Ramah, it was of sufficient size that 30 persons could be seated at a table, for that was where Samuel held the feast for Saul and his servant.

Samuel had instructed his staff to set aside a special "piece of meat" (v. 23) to give to Saul as his "share" of the sacrifice. In so doing, Samuel was treating Saul as if he were a fellow priest. All these arrangements, from Saul and his servant being seated at the head of the table, to his being served the special part of the sacrifice (Hebrew *shoq*, which could be rendered either "leg" [9:24] or "thigh" [Leviticus 7:33]), a part of the sacrifice distinctly reserved for the priestly cast.

After this festive meal was ended in the sacred area, Samuel, Saul and his servant went back to the "roof," perhaps of Samuel's house (v. 25), for further conversation. The next morning, Samuel instructed Saul to send his servant on ahead for a time, as he talked privately to Saul with a word he had received from the Lord for him (v. 27).

The Signs of Assurance God Would Give to Saul – 10:1–8

Numerous scholars view Saul's rise to kingship as consisting of three steps: He was first anointed by Samuel (9:1–10:16), later chosen by lot (10:17–27), and finally confirmed by public acclaim (11:1–15). This constitutes one of the more difficult problems in this account: the sequencing of the events and the relationship between 11:14–15 and 10:17–27—especially 11:14, "Come, let us go to Gilgal and there *reaffirm* the kingship." It is this last statement that gives us the most compelling evidence that this account of events from chapters 8–15 is one composed of several episodes put together. The best and simplest explanation, though, is that the meaning of this debated phrase just examined is that it is not speaking of Saul, but of the peoples' renewal of allegiance to God and his covenant. It is a call for a renewal ceremony that is given fuller detail in chapter 12.

Since the Lord had informed Samuel that he was to anoint Saul as king, he moved forward with that command and especially to tell Saul this anointing was from the Lord. The oil Samuel used to anoint Saul was made from a unique formula, not used for any other formula or occasion (Exodus 30:23–33). Even though Samuel felt he had been rejected by the people, as Saul was now put in his place of appointment, he still finished the ceremony by kissing Saul out of respect for God's appointment (10:1). This symbolized the coming of the Holy Spirit in power in this one who was declared "leader/ruler" (*nagid*) rather than "king" (*melek*). This was the first sign.

The second sign was that when Saul left Samuel that day, he would meet two men near Rachel's tomb at Zelzah on the border of Benjamin, who would tell Saul the donkeys had been found and his father was now more worried about his son than about the lost donkeys (10:2). Samuel told Saul to go on until he came to the "great tree of Tabor." There he would meet three men on their way up to Bethel, and they would greet him. One of them would be carrying three young goats, another three loaves of bread, and the other a skin of wine (v. 3). The three men would greet Saul and offer him two loaves of bread, which Saul was to accept (v. 4).

Then Saul was to go to Gibeah of God (apparently so-called because a high place could be found in connection with it), where there was a Philistine outpost, and he would receive the third sign (10:5–7). As he approached this town, he would meet a procession of prophets coming down from the high place playing lyres, tambourines, flutes and harps and prophesying. At that time, the Spirit of the Lord would come upon Saul in great power, and he too would prophesy with them; in fact, Saul would be changed into a different person (vv. 5–6). Once these signs were fulfilled, Samuel said, "do whatever your hand finds to do, for God is with you" (v. 7).

At a later time, Samuel would meet Saul at Gilgal, where Saul had been told to go and to wait for Samuel's arrival (v. 8). When Samuel arrived, he would offer burnt and fellowship offerings, but Saul was to wait "for seven days until I come to you and tell you what you are to do" (10:8b).

The Sign of the Holy Spirit Coming on Saul in Power – 10:9–16

"As Saul *turned* to leave Samuel, God changed Saul's heart and all these signs were fulfilled that day" (10:9). The Hebrew literally says Samuel "turned his shoulder"; it is translated "backs" in context. When he did this, just as Samuel had predicted in the third sign, God changed Saul's heart! Accordingly, when Saul and his servant arrived at Gibeah of God (also known as Geba or modern Jeba; v. 5), the Spirit of God came on Saul in power, and Saul joined the prophetic band as they acted ecstatically as he too prophesied! This site was some four miles north of Gibeah (modern Tell el-Ful), Saul's hometown. As news spread of his arrival, and that he had been anointed as "leader" by Samuel, the people turned out in great numbers to see this local boy who was the "son of Kish" (v. 11). What struck these townsfolk as so unusual was that they saw him prophesying with the other prophets (v. 11). That is what led to the universal question on all lips, which became a "saying/proverb" in their day (Hebrew *mashal*) in Israel: "What is this that has happened to the son of Kish? Is Saul also among the prophets?" (v. 11c)

As if to answer this proverb/parable that was being parroted abroad, one man, who also lived there, chimed in by answering the question: "And who is his father?" (v. 12). This is how this question became a saying of scorn in Israel (see 19:24)! After Saul stopped prophesying, his uncle (his father's brother) asked, "Where have you been?" (v. 14). Saul replied, "Looking for donkeys ... but when we saw they were not to be found, we went to Samuel [the prophet]" (v. 14b). Saul's uncle followed up with another question: "Tell me what Samuel said to you." Saul answered correctly, but only in part, "He assured us that the donkeys had been found." However, Saul did not mention anything about Samuel's discussion with him about the kingship (v. 6). This uncle, though unidentified here in this context, may well have been Ner, the father of Abner, who later commanded Saul's army (14:50–51).

Conclusions

1. It is curious how the Scriptures tie in the loss of Kish's donkeys with the appointment and anointing of Saul as new leader of Israel.

2. The signs that accompanied the story of the finding of the donkeys and the anointing of Saul as king confirm the fact that all this was the powerful work of God and his Spirit. Our Lord was using the lowly things and persons of this world to show his glory and might.

3. God had instructed Samuel the prophet the day before Saul arrived that he would send on the morrow the man he was to anoint as leader over the people of Israel—namely, Saul.

4. Even though Israel had rejected both Samuel and the Mighty Lord as the ones who led Israel, nevertheless the Lord had heard their cry for relief from their oppressor, so he announced that Saul would deliver his people from the hand of the Philistines.

5. Samuel seated Saul as the guest of honor with some thirty persons at a festive meal in his hall. Samuel took the choice piece of meat, the leg, and placed it in front of Saul.

6. Samuel walked with Saul and his servant down the hill from Ramah, then he asked the servant to go on ahead of the two of them, whereupon he poured a flask of oil on Saul's head, kissed him and announced: "The LORD has anointed you as leader of his inheritance."

7. Despite the number of signs given to various persons, the fact that Saul was God's choice for a new king only became clear as all the signs were combined.

Lesson 8

Samuel Uses the Lot in Choosing Saul as King and Nahash, the Ammonite King, Eyes a Way to Disgrace Israel

1 Samuel 10:17–27, 11:1–15, 12:1-25

Even though 1 Samuel 9:1–10:16 speaks of a previous private anointing of Saul, Samuel the prophet, in 10:17-27, deals more with the public choice of a leader that confirmed the prophet's earlier private action. In order to have this public confirmation, Samuel summoned the people of Israel to gather at "Mizpah," which is probably modern Tell en-Nasbeh, a site about eight miles north of Jerusalem on the road to that city.

Samuel began this specially called public convocation by reminding the people that the Lord had once again announced that it was he, and he alone, who had brought the nation up out of Egypt and from all the other nations that had oppressed them since that day; however, they had by their willful motives called for a king to rule over them, thereby rejecting the Lord, even though he had delivered them out of all their calamities and former distresses. Indeed, Samuel had made that very same point previously, for instance in 8:6–22. Nevertheless, Samuel proceeded with the casting of lots to determine who should be Israel's king just as the people had so fervently wanted it to happen. God's prophet took the nation through the process of the casting of lots, until he gradually he narrowed it down to "the man God" he had spoken to Samuel about in a private conversation (10:20–21).

First to be chosen by lot was the tribe of Benjamin, then as the lots proceeded through the clans of Benjamin until the clan of Matri was picked out of all the other clans (v. 20), and finally Saul the son of Kish was the person selected by lot, for indeed the lot, which would appear to many as being random, was from the Lord. Such a procedure seemed to be necessary in this situation especially, as Matthew Henry pointed out:

> Samuel also knew the peevishness of the people. And that there were those among them who would not acquiesce in the choice if it depended upon his [Samuel's] single testimony, and therefore, that every tribe and every family of the chosen tribe might please themselves with having a chance for it [the title], he calls for them to the lot. ... By this method it would appear to the people ... that Saul was appointed of God to be king. ... It would also prevent all disputes and exceptions.

Henry went on in that same context to correctly observe:

> When the tribe of Benjamin was taken, they might easily foresee that they were setting up a family that would soon be put down again; for the dying Jacob had, by the spirit of prophecy, entailed the dominion [of kingship] upon Judah" (Gen 49).[1]

But even though the lot had fallen on Saul, when the people searched the crowd that was with them for the man just chosen by the lot, Saul was not to be found among them (10:21). Therefore, it was necessary to ask the Lord, "Has the man come here yet?" (10:22a).

The Lord knew the answer, of course, and he answered: "Yes, he has hidden himself among the baggage." (10:22b). Some think God is not concerned with the little things in life, which we might regard as mere trivia, but what about this example of his knowledge as to where Saul had gone to hide? It shows our Lord knows everything, even what we might regard as little stuff and trivia. So, the people ran to the baggage area and there they found their man hiding among the baggage. So, they brought Saul out from among all the bags to stand before all the people! And "find" in this chapter!

What motivated Saul to hide among the baggage, we do not know; the text does not comment. Some commentators argue that it was a

---

1. Matthew Henry, *Commentary on the Whole Bible, 6 Vols.* (New York: Revell, 1975), 2:334, as cited by Dale Ralph Davis, *Looking on the Heart: Expositions of the Book of 1 Samuel 1–14, Vol. 1* (Grand Rapids: Baker Books, 1994), 103–14.

case of modesty, while other interpreters argue that here was a man who clearly was too timid and totally overwhelmed by the thoughts of accepting this task of being Israel's king. The point, however, was this: The Lord knew where he was all that time!

As Saul emerged from his hiding place, Samuel observed to the people: "Do you see the man the LORD has chosen? There is none like him among all the people!" (v. 24). That was quite a commendation, especially from a prophet so vehemently opposed to any idea of choosing a king like those of other nations! But with this public statement by Samuel the people seemed to agree with Samuel, for they all shouted: "Long live the king!" (v. 24b)

After the people had joined in an acclamation of the new king, Samuel once again outlined the "regulations of the kingship" (Hebrew *mishpat hammelukah*), as he had solemnly warned them would be the case if they chose a king (see 8:10–18). Some commentators incorrectly want to see two different sets of "regulations" here, but the fact that Samuel said he got all his words from the Lord proves that God was consistent with himself (8:10). Thus, the very equation of 8:9, 11 with 10:25 is exactly what the LXX version made long ago. The rights and duties of the king are what Samuel was instructed by the Lord to write in a book, which was laid before the Lord in the Tabernacle (10:25), just as the custom was observed for other important matters (cf. Exodus 17:14, Isaiah 30:8).

Samuel urged all the people to return home (10:25). So Saul went to his home, called "Gibeah of Saul" (11:4; 15:34), a.k.a. "Gibeah in Benjamin" (13:2, 15j; 14:16). "Gibeah" meant "hill" or "height" and was the modern site of Tell el-Ful, about three miles north of Jerusalem. This site was excavated by William Foxwell Albright in 1922 and again in 1933, which proved to be an Iron I site as history also led us to expect.

Not everyone was all that happy with the choice of the new king. Some "troublemakers" (or "wicked men" in the Hebrew), scoffed: "How can this fellow save us?" They outright despised Saul and "brought him no gifts" (v. 27), "but Saul kept silent," a reading that is in accord with the Dead Sea Scrolls reading found in 4QSamuel and the LXX.

However, very soon after this, God would test the nations and its new king Saul with an attack from the Ammonite king Nahash. Let us examine that text to see the results of what had just taken place.

Nahash, an Arrogant Troublemaker, Sets His Terms – 11:1–3

Israel faced a new source of trouble. This time it was from the Ammonite king Nahash, who lived on the east side of the Jordan River. Nahash besieged Jabesh-Gilead, a fortified city two miles east of the Jordan River situated on the Wadi Yabis. In fact, this hostile troublemaker must have been stirring up as much oppression and terror east of the Jordan as he could, for this was what Josephus also appeared to confirm in his *Antiquities* (VI.v.1 [68–70]). This is confirmed in one of the best-preserved Biblical scrolls from Qumran's cave number 4, where this additional text was found added to 1 Samuel 11:1 which said:

> Now Nahash, the king of the Ammonites, had been oppressing the Gadites and the Reubenites grievously, gouging out the right eye of each of them and allowing Israel no deliverer. [There were] no men of the Israelites, who were across the Jordan [that] remained, whose right eye Nahash, king of the Ammonites, had not gouged out. But seven thousand men had escaped from the Ammonites and entered into [the city of] Jabesh-Gilead.

This material may well have dropped out at some stage in the transmission of the text, but either way, Nahash was on a path of terror to make sure no other group of peoples could attack him, for it was known that the left eye was usually covered by a shield when the men were in battle, and thus with the loss of their right eye, the men were rendered useless in battle. Nahash also wanted to heap up as much disgrace and humiliation on his enemies as possible, for he must have judged Israel to be weak at that time.

Nahash means "snake" in Hebrew; biblical scholar Frank Cross said it is a shortening of *Nahash-tob*, meaning "good luck," where the verb is taken to mean "to practice divination." Anyway, the king said, "I will make a treaty with you only on the condition that I gouge out the right eye of every one of you and so bring disgrace on all Israel" (11:2). Jabesh's elders asked of him, "Give us seven days so we can send messengers throughout Israel; if no one comes to rescue us, we will surrender to you" (v. 3). So certain of himself was this ruthless ruler that on being asked to see if anyone in Israel would come to their rescue, he boldly granted the request! Nahash saw Israel as weak and completely unable to defend itself; further, he wanted to heap as much "disgrace" (Hebrew *herpah*, "scorn, mockery") on Israel as possible. Such hatred, arrogance and just plain chutzpah is all too often seen in such scornful monarchs.

When the messengers came from Jabesh-Gilead to Gibeah of Saul and told what the stringent terms for their deliverance were, the people all began to weep aloud and to mourn bitterly. King Saul was not there at the time, but when he came in from plowing in the fields with his oxen, he asked what all the crying and commotion was all about (11:5). Upon hearing Nahash's outrageous terms for the deliverance of the Israelite town Jabesh-Gilead, "the Spirit of God came upon him in power and he burned with anger" (v. 6).

Saul, the Man on Whom the Spirit Rushed in Power – 11:4–13

The people recognized their weakness and inability to meet such a challenge as Nahash had arrogantly raised. This power of the Spirit had come upon Saul once before, when he had experienced a time of "prophesying" with the little combo he had met up with on his way home from just being told he was the anointed king (10:6–10), but this was different and more in line with what all the Judges had experienced from the time of Judge Othniel (Judges 3:10) to the time when Judge Samson (14:19), who had led the tribes of Israel. God by his Holy Spirit filled Saul with a divine indignation and equipped him with might and power to be the military leader needed for that occasion. Such an outpouring out of the Holy Spirit in the Old Testament days was often accompanied by the anointing of the person to certain significant positions of leadership in Israel.

To show that he meant business, Saul cut his two oxen into twelve pieces and sent them as a symbol of what would happen to anyone's oxen in Israel who did not follow him and Samuel (11:7). That action was sufficient to strike into the hearts of all the people a real terror, so that they turned out *en masse*. Their response also may been one of curiosity, for they must not have believed that a man they regarded as very meek, who hid himself at his installation as a leader, would now be so assertive and dynamic. But what they did sense was the mighty power of the Lord was certainly present and at work in Saul. The troops assembled at "Bezek" (modern Khirbet Ibziq), some 17 miles west of Jabesh-Gilead, with an army numbering 300,000 men and another 30,000 from Judah. Scholars debate whether *'elep*, the Hebrew word for "1,000," should instead be rendered "a military unit," "tribe" or a "thousand"; there is insufficient evidence to say one way or the other. It just seemed to some that 330,000 seemed too large a number for that period of time. There are no actual facts to prove or disprove it from collateral sources or types of evidence.

Bezek was the very same place, where at the beginning of the period of the judges, two Israelite tribes had joined together to rout the Canaanites and Perizzites (Judges 1:4–5). Thus it seemed natural to choose Bezek as the staging ground for this new battle of the new king against the Ammonites.

Saul informed the messengers from Jabesh-Gilead to encourage the horror-stricken citizens of that city that divine deliverance was on the way (11:9). In fact, by the time the sun had gotten hot on the morrow, the beleaguered people would be saved from the threats of Nahash. This desperate people received this with enormous joy and great jubilation (v. 9b). But to the Ammonites, the messengers who had been sent to Gibeah were to say: "Tomorrow we will surrender to you, and you can do to us whatever seems good to you" (v. 10). That took some great confidence in the promise of help from the Lord, for this turned out to be the inaugural test of the new leadership. Perhaps there was a pun in what they were told to tell the Ammonites; instead of the enemy gouging out the eyes of the citizens of Jabesh-Gilead, the Ammonites could do what was good 'in their own eyes' (see the same pun in 14:36). That was a real poke in the eyes to the Ammonites!

There was little time to waste. Saul divided his men into three different groups to prepare for the attack. With this option, the troops had more mobility and also avoided the risk of losing the whole Israelite army if they faced an overwhelming enemy attack. Therefore, that night during the third watch of the early-morning timing, which saw the change from the darkness of night into the early vestiges of the dawn breaking on the horizon, Saul and his army attacked the Ammonites and caught them by complete surprise, thereby scattering them into every direction.

The rout of the Ammonites was so great that some in Saul's army said to Samuel, "Who was it that asked, 'Shall Saul reign over us?' Bring these men to us and we will put them to death!" (11:12). Immediately King Saul intervened with these words: "No one shall be put to death today, for on this day, the LORD has rescued Israel."

The Renewal of the Kingdom Reaffirmed – 11:14–15; 12:1–25

Following the tremendous victory over Nahash, Samuel called for the nation of Israel to gather at "Gilgal," near Jericho. There the people were to "reaffirm" the kingdom. Thus, the nation gathered at Gilgal and there they "confirmed Saul as king in the presence of the LORD" (11:15). All of this took place as part of the celebration of the overwhelming victory over boastful Nahash. It is true, of course, that Saul had already been appointed earlier as king at Ramah (10:1) and chosen by lot later at Mizpah (10:17–25). Now on this third occasion, the third and final stage in his rise as monarchy over Israel, the people of Israel were summed to Gilgal to "reaffirm" (Hebrew *hadash*, "to reaffirm, to make new, to renew," or "to be new") Saul's acclamation as king. The people greeted this invitation from the prophet Samuel to reaffirm the kingship with great enthusiasm in light of the just-concluded demonstration of his winning leadership and victory over Nahash. Once again, just as with the earlier ceremonies of covenant confirmation, fellowship offerings were used as the proper response from the people of the land (Exodus 24:5). Now Saul's ascent to the throne of Israel was complete.

Chapter 12 is now used to complete Saul's ascension to the throne, a story that has stretched from 1 Samuel 8 up to chapter 12, and a story that sets chapter 12 as a defining moment in Israel's history. Here, at the conclusion of the conquest and the end of the period of the Judges, chapter 12 marks the turning point towards what is known as the Deuteronomic Period of Israel's history, which will last until the end of the monarchic period.

The division of chapter 12 into three parts can be seen in the writer's use of the Hebrew conjunction and particle we'attah, "and now," in verses 2, 7 and 13, as noted by Dale Ralph Davis.[2] Accordingly, three distinct subsections can be found in chapter 12. They will be:

Samuel Vindicates His Covenantal Faithfulness – 12:1–5

Samuel began his apologia for his days of leadership by noting that he had done everything the people had requested of him as he gave them a "king" as their leader. He could not hide the fact hat he was getting old and gray.

Samuel Summarizes the Righteous Acts of the Lord – 12:6–12

Samuel now turned to rehearse the righteous acts of the Lord on behalf of Israel's history. He pointed out how God had appointed Moses and Aaron to bring them out of Egypt to settle down in Canaan. But the people of Israel soon forgot the Lord. The story during the time of the Judges was the same; for example, the Lord gave them over into the hands of Sisera, king of Hazor, and into the hands of the Philistines and the king of Moab, for Israel had once more forsaken the Lord. But this pattern was repeated over and over in Israel: First Israel would be in a crisis, then she would cry to the Lord for help, then he would raise up a leader to deliver them. For instance, the Lord sent such leaders as Jerub-Baal, Bedan (?) = Barak(?),[3] Jephthah and Samuel. In each case the pattern was repeated!

---

2. Dale Ralph Davis, *Looking on the Heart*, 120.
3. The reference to Jerub-Baal (meaning "let Baal contend," Judges 6:32) is an alternate name for Gideon, who turned down an offer to lead a dynastic rule in Israel. Barak was Deborah's general who beat Sisera (Judges 4:6–7) and Jephthah (Judges 11:1) was the Judge who conquered the Ammonites, who had sided with the Philistines. Last of all is Samuel, the last of the Judges.

Samuel Sets Out the Alternatives for the People – 12:13–25

Many regard verse 13 as the hinge verse for the whole chapter, one in which the permissive will of God gives the people what they have asked for over and over again, though they did not deserve his mercy and grace! Accordingly, if the people and the king would "fear the LORD" and serve and obey him, without rebelling against him, all would go well. But if they did not obey the Lord and there came a rebellion against the Lord and his commandments, God's hand would surely be against them, as his hand had been against their fathers (12:14–15).

On that same day, Samuel commanded the people to "stand still and see the great thing the LORD will do before your eyes" (v. 16). The wheat harvest was a time of the year when there never was any rain expected, when Samuel called upon the Lord, he did send "thunder and rain." This event was not only totally unexpected at this time of the year, but it came as a sign of the Lord's great displeasure with them (v. 17). In this manner, Israel could realize what an evil thing they had done in demanding a king ahead of time God had set and because of their wrong motives and reasons (v. 17b). The people were stunned and amazed at such an extraordinary thunder-storm with rain that had happened as a result of Samuel's calling on the Lord to send upon the nation this sign precisely during the harvest season. The people pled with Samuel to pray to the Lord so that they might not die, for they now realized that this demand for a king only added to the host of other forms of evil they had already done (v. 19).

Samuel encouraged the people by saying that even though they had done an evil deed in rejecting the Lord and asking for a king, they should not turn away from the Lord but "serve [him] with all your heart" (v. 20). Forget about serving "useless idols;" instead, serve the "great name of the LORD" and don't reject his people, for the Lord has been "pleased to make you his own" (v. 22b). As far as Samuel's future was concerned, he would not sin against the Lord by "failing to pray for you [the nation]" in days to come (v. 23). Moreover, he would "teach" them "the way that is good and right" (v. 23b). Israel, however, was to fear the Lord and serve him faithfully with all [their] heart" (v. 24), for surely they should reflect on "the great things [God] had done for [them]." But they were to also be sure that if Israel persisted in doing evil, both they and their king would be "swept away" (v. 25).

Conclusions

1. The Israelites had concluded that Samuel was now getting too old to rule over them and that his sons were themselves not walking in the ways of the Lord as Samuel had, so they were not the solution to the problems the nation was facing.

2. Israel demanded they be given a king so they could be like the other nations. This rejection, of both the Lord and Samuel, caused Samuel great grief and sorrow, which he poured out in his prayers to heaven.

3. Saul was privately identified as the future king at Samuel's hometown of Ramah, then he was chosen by lot to be the king at the town of Mizpah, and finally was reaffirmed to be that king at Gilgal as the people celebrated the fantastic victory over the Ammonites.

4. The arrogant boast of King Nahash of the Ammonites that he would gouge out the right eye of every citizen of Jabesh-Gilead became the occasion for Saul to be led under God to obtain a smashing victory and gain the confidence and support of the nation.

5. Samuel promised not to sin against God by not praying for the people who had rejected him and the Lord as well, in favor of a king. Faithfulness to the Lord required such an action, but personal feelings were not to displace this priority that obedience deserved.

Lesson 9

The Sad Decline of King Saul

1 Samuel 13:1–14:46

The sad story of Saul's decline appears mainly in 1 Samuel 13–15; David replaced Saul as king, and David's story begins in chapter 16 and continues through the rest of the book. During this time, Saul's successes tend to lessen and continue to go downhill, while those of David, the shepherd boy from Bethlehem, continue to rise and feature success after success.

Chapter 13 begins with Saul's age when he became king and the length of his reign, but these numbers are missing from the Hebrew text. Sadly, of the four Dead Sea Scrolls of the Samuel manuscript found at Qumran, 1 Samuel 13 is the only chapter missing in all four manuscripts. So the Hebrew text of 13:1 reads: "Saul was ... years old when he began to reign; and he reigned ... two years over Israel." Somewhere in the transmission of this text, the numbers dropped out, so we don't know what it said originally.

The story in chapter 13 begins with Saul choosing 3000 men to be his associates; perhaps they were regarded as his standing army. Two thousand went with Saul to the Philistine outpost of Michmash (modern Mukhmas), while one thousand men were put under the command of Jonathan (whose name means "the LORD has given"); the smaller contingent of men remained at Saul's capital and hometown of "Gibeah in Benjamin," modern Tell el-Ful, three miles north of Jerusalem (13:2). The site of Michmash was about four miles northeast of Gibeah in Benjamin. Saul felt the size of two thousand men in his army was adequate for the challenge he faced with the Philistines on this post, so he had apparently sent the rest of the troops home (v. 2c), but it was Jonathan who, with his smaller unit of men, started the war against the Philistines, and that is what brings us to this text.

Jonathan Starts a War with the Philistines – 13:2–15

Surprisingly, Jonathan, not Saul, instigated this war with the Philistines. Jonathan was not the king, just the king's son! Jonathan and his armor-bearer showed more courage and trust in the Lord as they started this war by bravely attacking an outpost of the Philistines at "Geba" in Benjamin (13:3), also called "Gibeah of God" (10:3), five miles north-northeast of Jerusalem. It would appear, then, that Jonathan was marked by characteristics of a greater boldness and trust in the Lord than his father showed.

When Saul realized something was stirring in the Philistine camp, even though he was still yet unaware what his son was up to, he had the ram's horn sounded throughout Israel to gather a larger army to face what was stirring up the Philistine camp, to which the people of Israel rallied. The word that went throughout Israel was that "Saul has attacked the Philistine outpost and Israel had become a stench to the Philistines" (13:4). The troops of Israel assembled at Gilgal, but there was no mistaking the point that the Israelites greatly feared the Philistines.

Saul recalled Samuel's earlier command about waiting (10:8), so he waited seven days for Samuel to arrive. Perhaps it was on the seventh day itself that Saul decided Samuel was not coming, or if he were, it would be too late, for things seemed to be falling apart already! So Saul decided to seek the favor of God all by himself, for his men, now "quaking with fear," were slowly beginning to drift off and scatter everywhere (13:7–8). He ordered the burnt-offering and the fellowship-offering be brought to him as king (v. 9). Just as he had completed making this offering to God, Samuel arrived, and Saul went out to greet him.

Samuel asked him right then and there: "What have you done?" (13:11). Some think Saul sinned by assuming the role of a priest in offering the sacrifices, yet that does not seem to be the point of Samuel's rebuke, for Samuel did not condemn him for that. Furthermore, David (2 Samuel 24:25) and later Solomon (1 Kings 3:15), in their roles as kings, both offered the same types of sacrifices to the Lord, yet there came no reprimand from God. Saul, however, sinned precisely because he clearly disobeyed the word of God given him by Samuel!

Some have a difficult time faulting Saul for his disobedience, for after all, he had waited perhaps seven days, and the Philistines' presence scared the daylights out of them, and they melted away until there were a mere 600 men left with Saul to face a very hostile enemy (13:15). But we don't know all the facts. On the other hand, neither do I think Samuel deliberately arrived late just to keep Saul on the defensive. We can understand the stress and pressure Saul was under, but he had to learn to trust God, even if that called for trusting the Lord even up to the last minute on the seventh day!

Samuel's conclusion of Saul's failure to wait for seven days was that the king had acted "foolishly" (Hebrew *sakal*, "to act foolishly in self-reliance"); he had "not kept the command the LORD [his] God gave [him]" (13:13). Moreover, had he indeed obeyed God's word, Samuel announced, "[God] would have established [his] kingdom (Hebrew *mamlakah*) over Israel for all time" (Hebrew `ad `olam; v. 13b)! That was a most significant statement!

At the same time, this promise presents Bible students with a difficulty. How is it possible to say Saul's house or dynasty could have ruled over Israel in perpetuity, when Genesis 49:10 had promised the kingdom specifically to the tribe of Judah long before Saul's reign, but not to the tribe of Benjamin from which Saul hailed? What is the answer to this mystery?

One attempted solution to this problem is that God did fully intend to give his kingdom to the house and rule of David, who would come from the tribe of Judah and presumably rule over just that tribe as the nation. On this view, the Lord then would have given Saul the rest of the northern tribes of Israel. Others compare the case of Saul with that of Jeroboam I, who in 1 Kings 11:38 was promised an "enduring kingdom" (Hebrew *bayit ne'aman*), similar to what David had been promised (e.g., in 1 Sam. 25:28; 2 Sam. 7:16), which would mean Jeroboam's kingdom would not replace David's but would exist in his northern kingdom of ten tribes alongside of the kingdom God would give to Judah and David! Others try to show that often Benjamin and

Judah were regarded by that time as one united tribe, but that hardly seems to relieve the problem! The real solution is known to the Lord, and we are left to guess and wait until we see our Lord.

Samuel twice reminded Saul that because he had not obeyed the Lord's command (13:13–14), God was searching for a man "after his own heart" (v. 14). Saul would be replaced by one of his neighbors who was a better man than he.

Samuel left Gilgal and went back to his hometown of Ramah. The LXX, however, had Samuel leaving Gilgal and going on his own way, while Saul and his troops went to Gibeah, which is in harmony with 1 Samuel 3:16.

Jonathan and His Armor-Bearer Cause a Philistine Rout – 13:16–14:23

The Philistines left camp as three different "raiding parties" (literally, "the destroyers"), one headed toward Ophrah, another toward Beth Horon, and the third toward the borderland overlooking the Valley of Zeboim (vv. 17–18).

At this point in the narrative, the writer felt it necessary to insert a note on how the Philistines had humiliated the Israelites by controlling all the blacksmiths working in iron, even in the jobs of sharpening the Israelites' agricultural implements. Despite these controls over anything made of iron, by God's power Jonathan was able to do great exploits even without the use of any iron implements (vv. 19–22). True, this humiliation was evident in the fact that there were no Jewish blacksmiths in the entire land of Israel; if Israel had blacksmiths, the Philistines determined, they could make swords and spears (v. 19). Therefore, everyone in Israel had to go abjectly down to the Philistine territory, later called the "Gaza Strip," to have their plowshares, mattocks, axes and sickles sharpened. The price charged by the Philistines was a "pym," two-thirds of a shekel in weight in silver, which turns out to be an exorbitant price for sharpening and repointing Israel's agricultural tools. In fact, such weights of money marked with this word *pym* on them have turned up at several excavations. Israel had few, if any, weapons such as swords or spears;

they were indeed heavily dependent on the help of the Lord. In fact, "On the day of the battle, not a soldier with Saul and Jonathan had a sword or spear" (v. 22). What a way to fight a war—unless the Lord was with them, they had no chance of winning!

A detachment of the Philistines had been sent out from their outpost in Michmash (13:16) to defend the pass leading to that military outpost (v. 23). Surprisingly, Saul's son Jonathan, not Saul, took the initiative to instigate the battle with the Philistines. Without telling his plans to his father, Jonathan and his armor-bearer planned to move out together. "Come, let's go over to the Philistine outpost on the other side," Jonathan said (14:1). He then proposed to his armor-bearer that they climb up the rugged cliffs, one called Bozez (which means "shining" because it faced north toward Michmash and caught the rays of the sun), and the other was called Seneh (which means "thornbush," perhaps because there were thornbushes growing on it; and it faced south toward Geba). These rocky crags appeared on each side of the pass leading up to Michmash.

As noted, Saul had meanwhile returned to his hometown of Gibeah, where he sat down on the outskirts of town under a pomegranate tree in Migron. Six hundred men were with him, including "Ahijah the priest," (whose name means "brother of the LORD"), who came from the rejected line of priests (in the line of Eli), wearing an ephod. He was the son of Ichabod's brother "Ahitub, the son of Phinehas, the son of Eli" (14:2). The divine judgment against Eli's house had been given earlier (2:30–33).

The armor-bearer was game on going with him to the Philistines' outpost; Jonathan had said, "Perhaps the LORD will act on our behalf. Nothing can hinder the LORD from saving, whether by many or by few" (14:6). So, the two set out to begin their climb up the sharp, rocky terrain.

Jonathan relayed his plan to his armor-bearer; "Come, then, we will cross over toward the men and let them see us. If they say to us, "Wait and we will come to you,' we will not go up to them, but if they say, 'Come on up," then we will keep on ascending this cliff, for this will be our sign from the LORD that he has given them into our hands" (14:8–9).

When the Philistines saw Jonathan and his armor-bearer, they mocked them, saying, "Look! The Hebrews are crawling out of the holes they were hiding in" (14:11). So the Philistines at the outpost yelled to them, "Come up to us and we'll teach you a lesson" (v. 12). That was the sign the two climbers were looking for, so they continued their climb up the two crags in what today is called Wadi es-Suweinit, a deep gorge seven miles northeast of Jerusalem that goes down toward Jericho. So, Jonathan climbed up the cliff using his hands and his feet with his armor-bearer right behind him (v. 13). When they arrived on top of the rocky crags, the two men killed twenty Philistine men in a space about a half an acre (v. 14).

A "panic sent by God" (v. 15) overspread the entire Philistine army, even those in the camp and in the field, for the ground itself shook, because of God's intervening work. This was enough to rouse Saul from his relaxed posture under the pomegranate tree outside of Gibeah. He ordered the troops be mustered at once to find out who was missing. When they had done so, they found out that Jonathan and his armor-bearer were the ones who had gone AWOL (v. 17).

Saul ordered the priest Ahijah to "bring the "ark of God" (v. 18), which happened to be with the Israelites at the time. While this was going on, the tumult in the Philistine camp increased more and more, so Saul ordered Ahijah to "withdraw your hand" and not bother asking God for directions anymore (v. 19). That was clearly a stupid act on Saul's part.

Saul then ordered the troops into battle, where they found the Philistines in complete disarray and in a total panic and confusion, striking each other with their swords. Meanwhile, the Jewish deserters, who had gone into hiding, or who had gone over to join Saul's army and had entered into the camp of the Philistine army, now switched back over to the Israelite army, when they heard the Philistines were on the run. Now they had rejoined Saul's army, they too joined in hot pursuit of these uncircumcised Philistine soldiers (vv. 21–22). "So on that day, the LORD saved Israel, and the battle moved on beyond Beth Aven" (v. 23; cf. Exodus 14:30).

The rest of the story of what happened that day is told in a flashback to the battle scene they had just faced in vv. 20–23. Earlier, Saul had foolishly bound the troops under an oath, requiring they abstain from eating any food for an entire day of the battle. But this resulted in the men growing "faint" and thus unable to press their advantage in the battle (14:28). However, when Saul's troops entered a forest, perhaps in the hill country of Ephraim, they noticed a honeycomb filled with honey[1] had fallen to the ground (v. 27), but they refused to taste the honey because of Saul's curse on anyone who ate. But Jonathan had not heard of this curse, so he dipped the end of his staff into the honey and ate some and his eyes were "brightened"; his strength was renewed at that moment. When one of Israel's fellow soldiers told Jonathan of his father's curse (v. 28), Jonathan remarked that his father "has made trouble" for the country, observing that had Saul not made such a foolish oath, a restrengthened army would have killed even more Philistines.

Even more frightening was the fact that on that same day as the battle took place, Saul's army "pounced on the plunder" (v. 31). They took it and butchered the sheep, cattle and calves right there on the ground and ate them together with the blood still in them. Since the evening had come, the men were no longer under Saul's oath of abstinence from eating (v. 32). When someone told Saul that the men were sinning against the Lord by eating meat with the blood still in it (v. 33), he was alarmed. Eating meat with blood still in it was forbidden by God (Leviticus 17:10–14; Deuteronomy 12:16, 23–24).

Saul rebuked his men for eating meat with blood in it, for by doing so they had broken and betrayed (Hebrew *bagad*) their promise to the Lord. Saul ordered that a large stone be rolled over to him and that the men be told that they were to slaughter the captured cattle and sheep on that boulder, for they had sinned against the Lord. So each man brought his ox and slaughtered it on the large stone. Then Saul built an altar to the Lord (v. 35).

---

1. See Ronald Youngblood, "1 and 2 Samuel," *The Expositor's Bible Commentary*, 149, note 27. He commented that in 2007, archaeologists discovered the first beehive colony from the biblical period of the mid-tenth to early ninth century B.C.E. The apiary had more than 30 hives at Tel Rehob, four miles from Beth Shan in the Jordan Valley.

On that day Israel had struck down the Philistines in a westward direction from Michmash all the way to Aijalon ("field of deer"), modern Yalo, sixteen miles west of Michmash and seven miles southwest of Upper Beth-Horon. Saul proposed they continue to go after the Philistines that night and continue to plunder them until dawn of the next day, but though the men were willing to do so, the priest Ahijah cautioned, "Let us inquire of God here" (v. 36c). But when Saul asked God if he should go down after the Philistines, God did not answer him that day! (v. 37)

Saul assumed the reason for God's silence was because there was sin in the camp, so Saul ordered the leaders of the army to come to him so he could find out what sin had been committed (v. 38). Saul even uttered an oath that even if he or his son were the guilty ones, they must die (v. 39). But no one said a word, for they all the army knew what was the matter, and who had broken the oath—Jonathan!

Saul had all the army stand to one side, and he and his son stood on the other side. The men showed their agreement to this division. Then Saul prayed to the Lord to give the right answer to the lot. The answer came, and Saul and Jonathan were chosen by the Lord, but the men were cleared. The lot was cast once again, and Jonathan was taken (v. 41). Saul demanded of Jonathan, "Tell me what you have done." So, Jonathan replied, "I merely tasted a little honey with the end of my staff. And now I must die?" (v. 43) Saul resolutely responded, "May God deal with me, be it ever so severely, if you do not die, Jonathan" (v. 44).

The army argued with Saul. However, saying, "Should Jonathan die—he who has brought about this great deliverance in Israel? Never! As surely as the LORD lives, not a hair of his head will fall to the ground, for he did this today with God's help" (v. 45). So the men rescued Jonathan, and he was not put to death. With that, Saul went back home and did not pursue the Philistines any more at that time (v. 46).

Conclusions

1. We do not know exactly where the battle described in chapter 13 came in the life of Saul's reign, but many put it somewhere near his mid-career.

2. When the Philistines assembled to fight Israel with their 3000 chariots and 6000 charioteers, it frightened the life out of Saul's small standing army of 3000 men, so all but 600 went off to hide, with some even crossing over to Trans-Jordania to be safe. In the meantime, Saul was to wait seven days until Samuel came—a command he disobeyed!

3. Jonathan and his armor-bearer decided to climb up either side of the pass leading to Michmash, where they killed 20 Philistines, which was accompanied by God sending a shaking of the ground that caused a terrific panic among all the troops of Philistia. The two men, Jonathan and his armor-bearer, believed God could save by a few just as well as by many.

4. Saul had uttered a curse on anyone who ate any food that day. But Jonathan, unaware of this, dipped his staff into a honeycomb, and his strength was renewed for the battle.

5. When Saul asked God if they should press the battle against the Philistines all that night, the Lord refused to answer him. Saul assumed this was because there was sin in the camp, so he searched who was the problem by lot, and his son Jonathan was selected by that lot. But the army spoke up and rescued Jonathan from dying.

Lesson 10

God Rejects Saul as King Over Israel

1 Samuel 14:47–54, 15:1–35

Before Scripture entered into the record God's rejection of Israel's first king, there was a brief accounting of some of the more brilliant moments in Saul's career in 1 Samuel 14:47–54. Presumably, most of this account is from the earlier part of his reign, perhaps about 1026 B.C.E., which we assume was about 40 or 42 years in length (13:1?). In those earlier days, Saul must have enjoyed enormous success, for he fought against an enemy on almost every side (14:47). Most commentators don't recognize that Saul was given an enormous amount of success at the start of his reign—perhaps for the first twenty years or so.

He was successful in facing the army of Moab, the attacks of the Ammonites, the army of Edom, the kings of Zobah, as well as the constant harassments by the Philistines (14:47b). In fact, the text said: "Wherever he turned, he inflicted punishment on [his enemies]" (v. 47c). Moreover, it is recorded, "He fought valiantly and defeated the Amalekites, delivering Israel from the hands of those who plundered them" (v. 48).

V. 49 gives the names of Saul's children. Three sons are listed: Jonathan (the firstborn), Ishvi (possibly the same person as Ish-Bosheth) and Malki-Shua. Unmentioned in this text is a fourth son, Abinadab. There were two daughters, Merab and Michal. Saul's wife was "Ahinoam daughter of Ahimaaz," but Saul also had a concubine, Rizpah, also not mentioned in this text (2 Sam. 3:7). Saul's cousin Abner was commander of the army. This note on Saul's family concludes by adding that Saul faced constant attacks from the Philistines for all the days of his reign (v. 52). Thus he was in constant need of brave men to join his ranks, and he constantly looked for such recruits (v. 52b)—not to mention, of course, the help he needed from God!

Let's look at this final time Samuel will bring the Word of the Lord to Saul.

Samuel Delivers the Message from God to Saul – 15:1–3

The prophet Samuel began his message for Saul by using the emphatic form of the personal pronoun, saying, "I am the one the LORD sent to anoint you" (v. 1). Samuel was God's chosen representative through whom he had not only anointed Saul as "king" over Israel, but also through whom God had declared his word to Saul (v. 1b). In this text, Saul is described here for the first time as being a "king" (*melek*), whereas previously he was described simply as a "leader" (*nagid*).

The message Samuel had for Saul was this: "Go, attack the Amalekites and totally destroy everything that belongs to them" (v. 3). The Amalekites referred to here were those who lived in the southern Negev of Canaan. They were the descendants of Esau through his son Eliphaz (Gen. 36:12, 15–17); 1 Chronicles 1:36). The reason for this divine command to "totally destroy" them was because of what the Amalekites had done to Israel as the people of God came up out of Egypt, when the Amalekites attacked the rear ranks of the line of march, killing off the elderly, the faint, the weary, the sick, the youngsters and those who could not keep up with the rest of the marching lines of the tribes of Israel, lagging behind because of their youth or because of their infirmities (v. 2). Amalek had attacked Israel even before they reached Sinai in their wilderness journey (Exodus 17:8–16). God's command was an order for Saul to bring on them complete destruction, for he used the verb "to totally destroy" (Hebrew *haram*) them seven times (15:3, 8–9 [two times], 15, 18, 20) and the cognate noun once (v. 21).

The verb "to totally destroy" has the idea of giving over irrevocable order to all the persons and possessions of those condemned to the Lord by liquidating everything in fire and utter destruction so nothing remained as loot or booty except those things fire could not destroy, such as gold, silver or iron. Those items must be put and kept in the house of the Lord. This word, though found elsewhere in the Bible, is used fairly often in this one chapter of the books of Samuel. All the uses of *haram* in 1 Samuel appear in the singular form except in v. 3, which uses the plural form, which meant Saul and Israel together were to attack the Amalekites in such a way that nothing would be spared; everything was either to be totally destroyed, i.e., put to death, and burned up, or if it was indestructible by these means, then it must be stored in the Tabernacle, regardless of what it was (Exodus 17:14–16; Numbers 24:20; Deuteronomy 25:17–19). The Amalekites clashed with Israel not only during the wilderness journey (Num. 14:43–45), but even after Israel had settled in the land; the Amalekites constantly invaded Judah's border (Judges 3:13, 6:33, 7:12, 10:12). They were corrupt to the core, and now their time of judgment had come, after such a long period of grace had been extended to them—some 400 years!

This call for a total annihilation of the Amalekites may not seem to us moderns to fit with God's character, but they refused to fear God (Deut. 25:18), so after waiting some 400 years for them to repent, God's patience ran out. Even he, who was seen to be "abounding in love and faithfulness," had a limit to what he would wait for a change from them (Exodus 34:6).[1] Had the Amalekites repented of their sin, things would surely have gone differently for them, but they did not turn!

Saul Prepares for His Battle Against the Amalekites – 15:4–9

Saul prepared for this attack by calling up all the men of Israel to muster at once at the site of Telaim, which is possibly Telem in the southern Negev. So, 200,000 foot-soldiers from Israel and 10,000 from Judah assembled as Saul's army, which appears to have dwindled since his battle with Nahash and the Ammonites (11:8)—or was the low number a sign of some of them being disaffected by Saul?

---

1. See Walter C. Kaiser, Jr., *Toward Old Testament Ethics* (Grand Rapids, MI: Zondervan, 1983), 74–75.

However, before Saul began this attack, he urged the Kenites living in or near the Amalekite towns to move out so they would not be killed, for they had "showed kindness" to the people of Israel centuries ago (v. 6), so they were now being spared any conflict or harm. So the Kenites moved away!

Then Saul's attack began against the Amalekites, for he went from Havilah (site unknown) to "Shur" (meaning "wall," perhaps the wall of Egypt, a site on the eastern border of the Nile Delta [v. 7]). This campaign covered an enormous area, so it may have taken some weeks to conclude.

Contrary to his instructions, Saul took Agag the Amalekite king alive, but all the people he destroyed along with the cattle and lambs—all but the best of the cattle and sheep (v. 8). However, the weak and despised cattle and sheep were "totally destroyed" by the army of Israel. Saul's failure to carry out God's word seems to come back later on in history to haunt Israel as Haman the Agagite (Esther 3:1, 10; 8:3, 5; 9:24) was described by the historian Josephus (*Antiquities* 11:21) as an Amalekite who tried to destroy all Jews in Persia on a day fixed by the casting of the lot (called the *pur*), perhaps in retaliation for Israel's partial destruction of his ancestors. "Agag" may also have been a royal title much like "Pharaoh."

It seems the army reassembled at the city named Carmel—not the Carmel of the north, but the one in southern Judah. There Saul set up a monument (Hebrew uses the word "hand" for "monument") to commemorate his victory (v. 12), but he set it up not to honor God, who gave the victory, but it "in his own honor" (v. 12). Then Saul and his men made their way to Gilgal, carrying with them the spoils of the selected cattle and sheep taken as booty from the enemy, and their trophy from the victory in the person of King Agag, the king of the Amalekites.

The Lord Tells Samuel He Is Sorry He Has Made Saul King – 15:10–21

The word of the Lord came to Samuel once again. However, this expression that "the word of the LORD came to" is used of God's word of revelation only three times in the books of Samuel: once of the blessing from Nathan the prophet to David (2 Samuel 7:4), and twice in a word of judgment, once through Samuel the prophet against Saul (1 Samuel 15:10) and once through the prophet Gad to David (2 Samuel 24:11).

God's word was that "I am sorry I have made Saul king, because he has turned from me and has not carried out my instructions" (v. 10). This upset Samuel tremendously when he heard these words, for the Lord himself had led Samuel to anoint Saul as leader of the people. How was it possible that God would set aside the very same man he had chosen to be king? Moreover, given the attacks that were coming on the nation, was this any time to be instituting a change in the government?

Early the next morning, Samuel began a painful walk from Ramah to meet Saul, but he was told that Saul had gone to Carmel to set up a monument to honor himself (v. 12). When Samuel arrived at Carmel, the people must have showed him Saul's monument, and he was told Saul had gone beck to Gilgal. So the aged Samuel retraced his steps and went to Gilgal across the hot sands of the dry lands.

When Samuel finally arrived at Gilgal, Saul, full of cheer and apparently in a celebratory mood, along with all the people, greeted him jubilantly. saying, "The LORD bless you! I have carried out the LORD's instructions" (13). Saul's conscience must have been bothering him, for he took the initiative by setting the tone for things up-front before he was asked whether he had "carried out the LORD's instructions." But that was precisely what he had failed to do!

Samuel, however, cut Saul short and retorted in effect, "If you have kept the LORD's instruction, then what is all the bleating of sheep and the lowing of cattle I hear?" (v. 14)

Saul had a ready answer: "The soldiers brought them [here] from the Amalekites; they spared the best of the sheep and cattle to sacrifice to the LORD *your* God, but we totally destroyed the rest" (v. 15). Did you note the word Saul slipped in there: "*your* God"? And who in heaven had made a such a distinction between the best and the weakest of the booty as Saul had just announced?

"Stop!" Samuel ordered Saul. Samuel was in no mood to entangle himself in an argument; Saul had failed miserably. That was that! Samuel proceeded to announce the tragic news the Lord had given him the previous night (v. 16): "[The LORD] has rejected you as king!" (v. 23d). Samuel was clear in his condemnation of Saul, even though his emotions must have been in turmoil at the time: Saul had disobeyed God by sparing Agag, and Saul had insisted that the sparing of the best of the flock was a sign of his doing what God wanted him to do. On the top of all the herds was the prime responsibility Saul had for the people themselves; anyway, he countered, some in these choice cattle and sheep were piously designated to be used in a sacrifice! But Samuel was not going to be taken in by Saul's sophistry and the people's pretense to be obedient. The Lord required wholehearted obedience, not half-hearted or partial obedience from king and people. The word given here became a classic text on the importance of obedience and on the proper motivation for making sacrifices to the Lord. One cannot and should not pit the sacrificial ritual over against or instead of the biblical emphasis on obedience; what is the use of performing the ritual if it did not come out of a heart of obedience?

Samuel's Condemnation of Saul's Disobedience – 15:22–35

These words must have struck terror into Saul's heart, for in the poetry of verses 22–23, God ranked him with idolaters and those who practiced witchcraft! The issue here was not an either/or situation; that is, the question was not whether to obey or to sacrifice, for the Lord does not delight or take pleasure in sacrifices or burnt offerings *per se*. He wishes to see the heart of obedience that prompts such ritual (Isaiah 1:11). Therefore, obedience and sacrifice go together if the heart attitude is right. Saul had already been rebuked by Samuel for his impetuosity and his disobedience, but now he was rebuked for his half-hearted fulfillment of God's directive. Thus, his rejection of the Lord's command led to the Lord's rejection of him! Samuel rebuked Saul with these words:

> Does the LORD delight in burnt offerings and sacrifices as much as in obeying the LORD? To obey is better than sacrifice, and to heed is better than the fat of rams. For rebellion is like the sin of divination is like the evil of idolatry. Because you have rejected the word of the LORD, he has rejected you as king!

When confronted with the Lord's verdict, Saul's immediate response was to try to mitigate his sentence, so he confessed:

> I have sinned. I violated the LORD's command and your instructions. I was afraid of the people and so I gave in to them. Now I beg you to forgive my sin and come back with me, so that I may worship the LORD. (vv. 24–25)

But it is clear that Saul's confession was not a real admission from his heart and sorrow over his sin, but more an evidence of his fear of losing the respect and acclaim of the people of Israel. Saul wanted more than anything else to be admired and respected by the people for his leadership abilities and for the way he had shown his military prowess in defeating so many nations. As a result of this earnest desire to be admired by them, he had "obeyed their voice" (15:24) instead of giving priority to the word of God.

When Saul saw that Samuel was about to leave, he begged him to return with him to the place of sacrifice so he might worship the Lord.

At first Samuel refused, saying, "You have rejected the word of the LORD, so the LORD has rejected you from being king over Israel" (v. 26). As Samuel turned to leave, Saul in desperation fell to his knees and grabbed the hem of Samuel's robe, which tore. With his torn robe in Saul's hand, Samuel used this act as a symbol and message to the king: *The Lord has torn the kingdom from your grip, and he has given it to someone more worthy of such a task.* Saul appealed to Samuel once again to accompany him so all the people would see that all appeared to be well in the eyes of his comrades, so Samuel went with Saul, perhaps somewhat reluctantly (v. 30).

Now that the celebration of the victory over the Amalekites was over, Samuel ordered Agag, the king of the Amalekites, be brought to him. Agag came to Samuel in a somewhat confident manner, thinking he was no longer under the threat of death. But Samuel put Agag to death there in Gilgal. As he did this, Samuel uttered these words: "As your sword has made many women childless, so will your mother be childless among women" (v. 33).

There was no longer any way to heal the breach between Samuel and Saul. Saul continued to rule as king for what may have been some fifteen years, but he no longer was God's representative, nor was his seed of descendants in line to possess and continue the kingdom of Israel he had once held. Saul apparently tried his best to earn once again the respect he had had by driving out of Israel all the witches and soothsayers (15:23; cf. 28:3). But it was all for naught and all too late! Chapter 15 closed with the sorrowful words: "And the LORD was grieved that he had made Saul king over Israel" (v. 35). The Lord was finished with Saul as king!

Conclusions

1. Samuel gave King Saul a word directly from the Lord, which said he was to punish all the Amalekites for what they had done to Israel during their wilderness wanderings some 400 years ago. There were to be no survivors, nor any booty, left that was not destroyed!

2. Saul carried out the Lord's directive, but he did give an advance warning to the Kenites who lived among the Amalekites to leave them so they were not affected by this war, for they had shown kindness to Israel in the past.

3. Saul did not completely obey the Lord, for he and his army spared Agag, king of the Amalekites, along with the best of the cattle and sheep owned by the enemy.

4. Because of this disobedience, the Lord was sorry he had chosen Saul as king. This divine remark caused Samuel to cry out to the Lord all night.

5. Samuel arrived in time to discover how Saul had disobeyed, so he was given the divine word that the Lord was not concerned with sacrifices as much as he was with the heart and obedience of the worshiped preceding that sacrifice.

6. Saul confessed his sin, but it was not a genuine confession; he was more concerned with how he looked and appeared to the people. This type of sorrow for sin is called "attrition," i.e., sorrow over being caught, but it was not "contrition," sorrow for having done such disobedient things.

Lesson 11

Samuel Anoints David as King

1 Samuel 16:1–23, 25:1–44

Samuel continued to grieve over the fact that the people had rejected him as their leader, but he was also grieved over the fact that the Lord had rejected Saul, the very man the Lord had personally chosen as king. That is why the Lord asked Samuel: "How long will you mourn for Saul, since I have rejected him as king over Israel?" (16:1)

Instead of continuing to mourn over the loss of Saul, Samuel was to "fill his horn with oil and be on [his] way" (v. 1b), for God had a new mission for him. God was sending him to Bethlehem, from there he had chosen one of Jesse's sons to be the new king. This he said plainly: "I [the LORD] have chosen one of his sons to be king" (v. 1c).

Samuel, however, was troubled with these instructions, for he was sure "Saul will hear about [my trip] and will kill me" (v. 1c). The Lord's answer to Samuel was to take a *heifer* with him and say, "I have come to sacrifice to the LORD" (v. 2). Now to get to Bethlehem, Samuel would have to pass by Gibeah, Saul's hometown, so what was he to say as an explanation for why he was on this trip? It was clear that Samuel was not on one of his scheduled ministerial-circuit stops listed on his ordinary places of leading worship in these various towns. His schedule was well-known to the folks of that area.

Still, Samuel was to go to Bethlehem with an offering as God had instructed. When he got to Bethlehem, he was to invite a man named Jesse to the sacrifice (v. 3). But what would Samuel say if Saul, or any of his cronies, asked why he was going to Bethlehem when he was not scheduled to be there at that time? That question could lead to a lot of trouble.

This is an important issue, for God appears at first to be telling Samuel to lie, or at the very least, to be somewhat deceptive about his purpose in going to Bethlehem. Is there any indication in the Bible that under certain circumstances God approves of concealing the truth, simply to accomplish some higher good, as some would argue?

To answer that question, we must first assert that it is always wrong to tell a lie, for Scripture does not give us any grounds for telling either an outright lie or even a "half-truth." But as John Murray correctly observed, Saul also had forfeited his right to know all the facts and the full story in this situation, because of his sinful failures, but that did not mean Samuel, or anyone else, thereby had the right to lie or deliberately deceive anyone.[1]

So what is the answer then? Note first that Bethlehem, the town Samuel was headed to, was a little village some six miles south of Jerusalem and about eleven or twelve miles southeast of Samuel's hometown of Ramah. In Bethlehem, Samuel was to anoint one of Jesse's sons as a king to replace the rejected king Saul. This event would infuriate Saul if he heard of it.

In the village of Bethlehem there lived a young shepherd boy named David, from the family of Jesse. David was the person the Lord had already chosen to be the next king. Here David makes his full appearance for the first time in 1 Samuel 16, but his story and appointment by God will extend into the rest of 1 and 2 Samuel as well. This section of Scripture from 1 Samuel 16–31 may be labeled "The History of David's Rise," and it will form part one of another one of our character studies in this series. The coming one will be *David: The Man After God's Own Heart.*

Thus, the narrative begins with Samuel receiving God's instruction in 16:1–13 to stop grieving and being so dejected over the divine rejection of Israel's first king Saul, whom Samuel had indeed helped appoint as king as directed by God; instead, the prophet was to go to Bethlehem, and there he was to anoint Saul's successor. But once this successor to the kingship of Israel was found, Samuel was not left without anything to do for a good while during the rest of Saul's reign;

---

1. John Murray, *Principles of Conduct: Aspects of Biblical Ethics* (Grand Rapids, MI: Eerdmans, 1957), 139–41. Also see Walter C. Kaiser, Jr., *Hard Sayings of the Bible*, 210–11.

instead, 6:14–23 relates how this successor, even though he came from such humble circumstances as one who tended the shepherd's fields, had nevertheless found his way immediately into the court of King Saul, by the mighty providential working of God.

In the earlier coronation of Saul, the initiation of the Israelite monarchy in chapters 8–15 began with the account of King Saul being anointed at the people's demand, so now the establishment of the monarchy under David begins with a series of narratives that show his slow rise to power. However, David's careful rise is closely connected with the parallel decline of Saul's tenure as king. Hence, the stories of Saul and David crisscross at several points in the rest of the chapters of 1 Samuel and thus make for some of the most exasperating, yet fascinating, portions of Scripture. But first, let us examine parts of chapter 16 to get the rest of the Samuel story.

David Anointed as King Over Israel by Samuel – 16:1–13

Chapter 16 continues where 15 ended with the prophet Samuel still mourning for Saul. So what was the prophet's problem? God comforted Samuel by telling him to let bygones be bygones. But perhaps Samuel was also grieving over the fact that he had not been a mentor to Saul; after all, Samuel had devoted a good deal of his life to instructing Saul, and it was he who had actually anointed him as king, when Israel demanded a king to rule over them like the other nations. But Samuel may have feared that with Saul's failure, the failure of the nation might not be far behind in time. Did this change in governmental leadership mean Israel's enemies would now take advantage of them, or would civil war break out over this little-known choice for their leadership? A shepherd boy as Israel's king? Really?

But the Lord clearly instructed Samuel to 'get over it.' He was to take "horn with oil" and go to a man named "Jesse of Bethlehem," for God had chosen one of Jesse's sons as the new king (v. 1b). Samuel obeyed, even though he was apprehensive as to what Saul would do if and when he learned why he, God's prophet, had gone to Bethlehem. As Samuel approached the gates of the town, the elders came to greet him and asked him somewhat apprehensively, "Do you come in peace?" (v.

4) Perhaps they too feared that someone in the village was guilty of an offense and that was the reason for the prophet's unscheduled visit! But Samuel quickly assured that he had indeed come in peace. Apparently, uppermost in their minds was their hearing of Samuel's recent execution of King Agag (15:33). But Samuel's calm answer eased their immediate anxieties. The elders were to consecrate themselves and come to the sacrifice Samuel would carry out (v. 5).

Recall that Samuel had been instructed to take a "heifer" with him as he traveled to Bethlehem and to lead in offering a sacrifice of that heifer (v. 2). Then he was to invite Jesse and the elders to the actual sacrifice, and from there on God would tell him what to do (v. 3).

The key word in chapter 16 is the word "see" (Hebrew ra'ah). The Hebrew root of this word appears nine times in the chapter.[2] In v. 1 the verb "see" is best translated as "chosen" in some of these word usages, as in the election of a king (cf. 2 Kings 10:3).

As Samuel followed God's instructions, however, he feared what Saul would do when he heard what he had come to do (v. 2). This is why the Lord had told him to take along a sacrifice of a heifer as a secondary reason for his making the trip and offer it as a fellowship-offering along with the ritual of anointing.

Samuel seemed eager to start the process of anointing a king (v. 6); almost as soon as he cast his eyes on the stately appearance and stature of Jesse's eldest son Eliab (meaning "my God is father"), Samuel felt certain that here was God's next anointed king. But the Lord rebuked him, saying,

> "Do not consider his appearance, or his height, for I have rejected him. The LORD does not look at the things man looks at. Man looks at the outward appearance, but the LORD looks at the heart." (16:7)

King Saul, their present king, was a full head and shoulders above the height of all the people, but if Samuel was using Saul's height as a measure of what he was looking for, he had incorrectly missed God's

---

2. It appears as a verb in vv. 1, 17, to "see" or "look at" in vv. 6, 7 , as nouns in vv. 7, 12, and three times as an "appearance" in v. 18.

real indicator for selecting a leader by God's standards. Eliab, Jesse's oldest and apparently his tallest, was not that man!

Next Jesse introduced his second and third sons, Abinadab and Shammah, to Samuel, but neither was the man God was looking for (vv. 8–9). As the process went on, Jesse introduced all seven of his sons to the prophet, but none were acceptable to the Lord (v. 10). Naturally, Samuel was baffled as to what was going on here, so he asked Jesse, "Are these all the sons you have?" (v. 11). To Samuel's great relief, he said no. "There is still the youngest, but he is tending the sheep." Samuel replied, "Send for him; we will not sit down [to eat] until he arrives" (v. 11d). The Hebrew word "youngest" can also be rendered "smallest," perhaps in deliberate contrast to David's oldest brother Eliab and to Saul's great height. In fact, a Hebrew pseudo-Davidic and non-canonical psalm from Qumran (11QPsa Ps 151) has David say:

> Smalle[r] was I than my brothers, the youngest of my father's sons. So, he made me shepherd of his flock. ... He sent his prophet to anoint me, Samuel, to make me great. My brothers went out to meet him, handsome of figure and of appearance. Though they were tall of stature, [and] handsome because of their hair, the LORD chose them not.

Accordingly, when Samuel had first met Saul, in the previous search for a king, he was looking for his father's lost donkeys (9:2–3), but when we first meet David in this new search, he was looking after his father's sheep; the metaphor of shepherding was much more conducive to learning how to rule over a people than searching for donkeys!

David was numbered the "eighth" child in 17:12–14; however, 1 Chronicles 2:13–15 lists Jesse's sons and calls David the "seventh," a position in the family order of birth, which Josephus also assigns to David. The solution to this puzzle must be that one of David's older brothers must have since died without offspring, was thus omitted from the genealogy of 1 Chronicles 2:13–15, and David was moved up in the birth-order.[3]

---

3. Walter C. Kaiser, Jr., *Hard Sayings of the Bible*, "Did Jesse have Seven or Eight Sons?", 239.

When David was finally brought to Samuel, he was seen as "ruddy" (Hebrew *'admoni*) of complexion and a man of "fine appearance" with "handsome features" (v. 12). Then the Lord said to Samuel, "Rise and anoint him; he is the one" (v. 12b). So Samuel took the "horn of oil" he had brought along and anointed David in the presence of his brothers. From that very day forward, "the Spirit of the LORD came upon (Hebrew *salach*, "seized") David in power,"[4] then Samuel left to return to his hometown Ramah (v. 13).

David Arrives in the Court of Saul – 16:14–23

From this point onward it seemed as if King Saul was also beginning to lose his ability to govern. First of all, we read that the Spirit of the Lord had by now departed from Saul and an evil spirit from God "terrified" or "terrorized" him (v. 14). It may well have involved a serious and actual disturbance in Saul's mental health, but the fact that it came right after the departure of the Lord's Spirit from Saul cannot be discounted and regarded as an incidental part of the episode. Was this disturbance the work of a demon, or was it more of a spirit of distress and calamity in King Saul?[5]

Saul's attendants asked him, in an apparent flashback in this story of David, if they could search for someone to play the harp for the king, for when this evil spirit settled over him, perhaps the music would soothe his soul and make him feel better (v. 15). When they were given permission for such a search, one of the servants volunteered that he knew someone who could really play the harp well; he was good-looking, and "the LORD is with him" (v. 18). Saul gave the approval to send for this man, who turned out to be none other than David, son of Jesse (v. 19). Note how God's providence was at work in all that was taking place, for this would position David precisely where he needed to be for his future work as he learned how Saul functioned as a king even without that fact specifically being told to Saul.[6]

---

4. See David H. Howard, Jr., "The Transfer of Power from Saul to David in 1 Samuel 16:13-14," *Journal of the Evangelical Theological Society*, 32.4 (Dec. 1989), 473–83, especially 477.

5. Walter C. Kaiser, Jr., Hard Sayings of the Bible, "I Sam 16:14, An Evil Spirit from the Lord," 211–12.

6. Walter C. Kaiser, Jr., Hard Sayings of the Bible, "Why Did Saul Ask [for] David's Identity?", 213–14.

At Saul's request, David was summoned to the king's quarters. As a send-off present to David and a gift for the king, Jesse loaded a donkey with gifts for David to take to Saul, which were full of bread, a skin of wine, and a young goat (v. 20). When David arrived at the king's court and began to play his "harp" (Hebrew *kinnor*)[7], Saul apparently "liked him very much" (v. 21)—at least at first. David also became one of Saul's armor-bearers, sort of a member of his CIA "secret service of the throne." Saul sent word to David's father Jesse asking permission for him to allow David to remain in his royal service, which was granted (v. 22). Thus, periodically, when the spirit of despair came over Saul, David would quickly take his harp and play in Saul's presence, and relief would come to Saul as a result of David's playing (v. 23). No wonder, then, that David gained the reputation of being "Israel's singer of songs" (2 Samuel 23:1). All of this became something for Saul to really "harp about."

The fact that God himself is said to have used an alien spirit to serve his divine purposes is seen elsewhere in the Old Testament, for on such occasions, I can also affirm this about God's people:

> "[They] were not very concerned with determining secondary causes and properly attributing them to the exact causes. Under divine providence everything ultimately was attributed to him; [so,] why not say he did it in the first place?"[8]

Prior to David's coming to Saul's court, his reputation must have been building around the rumors from his days of shepherding that he had killed both a lion and a bear (17:34–35), so that his bravery entitled him to be called a "mighty man of valor" (Hebrew *gibbor hayil*). Later, perhaps as a member of the local militia, he fought against marauding Bedouins, who from time to time perhaps had raided the villages, and so David was also known as "a man of war" (Hebrew *'ish milhamah*).

---

7. "What Did David's Lyre [Harp] Look Like?" *Biblical Archaeology Review* 8:1 (Jan/Feb 1982), 34. Of the 15 occurrences of Hebrew *niggen*, "play an instrument," it appears in this section: 16:16 (two times), 17, 18, 23; 18:10; 19:9.

8. Walter C. Kaiser, Jr., *Hard Sayings of the Old Testament*, 131.

David Loses His Best Friend Samuel – 25:1

Samuel, the prophet who had anointed David and had been his counselor on many an occasion, died at a good old age—between 92 and 96. David felt alone without Samuel's presence and prayer support in a most dramatic way. Israel, however, assembled together and came to mourn over Samuel's death (25:1). They buried Samuel at his home in Ramah (v. 1b). Some local traditions place Samuel's tomb in Nebi Samwil, a site northwest of Jerusalem, but that identification would depend on equating Ramah with Nebi Samwil, an equation we cannot be sure of. Clearly one point was true: This was a huge loss for David, for now he had to find other avenues of support, since Samuel was his chief supporter.

Israel, naturally, mourned for Samuel, now that he was dead, but such an attitude of respect for Samuel had not always been true during the prophet's lifetime. The nation preferred to follow King Saul rather than a prophet Samuel, which often meant the nation was usually the greater loser.

Conclusions

1. God instructed the prophet Samuel to go to Bethlehem and anoint one of the sons of Jesse; however, God did not at that point say which child that would be or what his name was.

2. Samuel was afraid that, given Saul's reputation for being jealous about his position, along with his seeming irrationality at times, that Saul would kill him if he found out he had anointed someone else to be king.

3. God told Samuel to take a heifer along to anoint a son of Jesse in Bethlehem, and should he be asked, he was to say he was going to offer a sacrifice, which of course was true. Was Samuel, or are we, required in all circumstances to tell all we know about a situation in order to be speaking truthfully? Samuel had no right to lie, but neither did Saul have a right to know everything that Samuel was up to!

4. Samuel completed his days of ministry in Israel even though he deeply regretted Saul's poor completion of his reign.

5. David's gift of music was also used in the providence of God to calm King Saul; however, David's demeanor seemed always to be balanced and predictable in his actions contrary to Saul's actions later in his life.

Questions for Thought and Reflection

1. Do you understand some of the reasons why Samuel mourned for such a long time over God's rejection of Saul as king? What was his problem?

2. Was Samuel guilty of preparing to give Saul, if he asked him, a partial truth as to why he was going down to Bethlehem at this unscheduled time? If so, is that being truthful?

3. Why did God hold back the name of which of Jesse's sons he had chosen to be king? What do you think he was trying to do with Samuel?

4. How do you explain the Spirit came upon Saul and later left him? How necessary is it to have the Holy Spirit if we are to do God's work or even carry out his call on our lives regardless of the work we do?

Lesson 12

Samuel Makes a Final 'Appearance'

1 Samuel 28:3–25 [1]

For the final, unexpected glimpse of Samuel, the scene shifts to the slopes of Mount Gilboa. The writer reminds us that Samuel had died some time ago and that Saul had expelled all mediums, necromancers and spiritists from the land (28:3). Saul watched in alarm as the Philistine forces rallied in large numbers for battle against Israel, so he in turn summoned all the army of Israel to his side as he set up camp at Gilboa. Meanwhile the Philistines set up camp at Shunem. But when Saul saw the size of the Philistine army, "he was afraid and terror filled his heart."

The Philistines had chosen the great Plain of Esdraelon as the place where they would fight Saul and his army. This broad, flat valley goes slightly downward toward the Jordan River and is hedged in on either side by two mountain ranges. On the south side of what was now a three-mile-wide valley were the mountains of Gilboa with the city of Jezreel on a slightly elevated spur and a spring that gushed down into a large pool of water (now visited by loads of tourists). On the north was Mount Moreh, where there was a village called Little Hermon with the village of Shunem at its base, along with another city, Endor, just north of Hermon.

This portion of Scripture indeed contains a very strange chapter, for it recounts how Saul in his desperation to get a word from the supernatural world, or from anywhere for that matter, especially when God refused to answer him by any of the traditional the ways (v. 6). So Saul went to a "witch," also called a "medium" or "necromancer" (v. 7), where he learned he would die in his last battle with the Philistines (28:19). What is going on here? Was this actually happening? If only

---

1. This chapter is a slightly revised and expanded chapter that also appears in the David "Character Study" in this same series.

Samuel were still alive, Saul could have had a clearer picture of what was happening and what he might do! But Samuel had died, so that option was no longer available.

This chapter in the life of Saul (as it also seriously affected David and Samuel) clearly traced the current problem Saul faced (28:4–6), Saul's search and subsequent conversation with the necromancer came first (vv. 7–14), followed by his amazing conversation with a recalled-from-the-dead prophet Samuel, who had just now been brought up from the grave (vv. 15–19), along with the story of Saul's final meal before his death (vv. 20–25). Let us go to this text and see if we can understand what is going on.

Tormented by No Answers from God – 28:4–6

This text begins by reminding us that the prophet Samuel had since died, and he had been buried in his hometown of Ramah (28:3; cf. 25:1). In the meantime, Saul had expelled all mediums and spiritists from the land in accordance with the teaching Moses and others had given on this topic in Leviticus 19:31; 20:6–7; Deuteronomy 18:9–22; Isaiah 8:19–20. What had so suddenly prompted this action, we are not told. Might it have been a desire on Saul's part to suddenly appear to be super-religious, after a period of time in which he showed an absence of his desire to follow the teaching of Scripture, or could it be that there was some other motivation?

Again the Philistines assembled their men for war and set up camp near Shunem (v. 4). This town (modern name Solem) was on the southern base of Mount Moreh, some nine miles east-northeast of Megiddo. It appears two other times in the biblical record: (1) as the town from which Abishag came, she who was the virgin who functioned as a warming pad for shivering and aged King David in his senior years (1 Kings 1:3), and (2) the hometown of the well-to-do woman who built a prophet's chamber on her flat roof for whenever the prophet Elisha passed through the area (2 Kings 4:8, 12). Over against these pagan Philistine forces and some ten miles south-southeast of Saul's army encamped at Gilboa was the site where Saul, his son Jonathan, and a large part of his army would lose their lives in the forthcoming battle.

When Saul "saw" the size and preparedness of the Philistine army, he became "afraid" (this may be a wordplay; both "to see" and "to be afraid" are spelled in *wyr'* in Hebrew; 28:5) and is best rendered as "terror filled his heart." Saul decided he had better ask of the Lord what to do, but no matter how he tried to get an answer, whether by dreams, by the Urim (the sacred lots stored in the priestly ephod), or by a word through one of the prophets, God would not answer him. This must have been a huge clue to him that not only was something perhaps going to be terribly wrong, but that the Lord had by now totally abandoned him just as he said he would.

Helped by a Necromancer of Endor – 28:7–14

Though Saul had purged the land of necromancers, mediums and spiritists, he ordered his men to find such a woman who possessed such skills, for he wanted to make some inquiries via the netherworld if the godly realm was not going to answer (28:7). Interestingly enough, Saul's men knew just where to find such a woman, despite Saul's order that they all be put out of business and killed. There was one at Endor (v. 7b). The term "spiritist" is from the Hebrew *yidd'oni*, meaning "one who has [occult?] knowledge") and is found with the word "medium." The word "spirit," which in Hebrew is *'ob*, rendered "ghost" in Isaiah 29:4, also seems to have a technical meaning of "one who consulted the dead on behalf of the living" (v. 8) But it too is a very difficult word to translate.[2]

That is perhaps how this chapter functions in the history of Israel, for it also leaves a telltale sign of how low Israel had gone in her falling away from the Lord God who loved them and had rescued them ever since their days of coming out from Egypt. It may be saying too much to say Saul had inquired of the Lord for an answer, for by now he had lived all too long without contact with the Lord—ever since Samuel gave up on him. In fact, Saul simply "asks" of the Lord, but

---

2. See Clyde E. Billington, "The Ghost Pits of Saul and Odysseus," *Artifax* 23.3 (2008), 17–18.

the verb used in the parallel passage in 1 Chronicles 10:14 is the Hebrew verb *drsh*, "to seek" the Lord.

This passage raises the question, *Does this Scripture also permit Christians today to try to contact the dead by means of mediums or necromancers to inquire of those who have gone on before us?* Absolutely not! But a second question follows: Did this chapter involve, then, a piece of fakery with no contact with reality and was absolutely false? Probably not, for when the woman saw Samuel emerge from his grave or appear as it were on the other side of eternity, she screamed at the top of her lungs for two reasons: (1) she probably was not in the habit of seeing such a unusual event as the "calling up" of Samuel from the dead actually work (v. 12a), and (2) she suddenly realized that her disguised client was none other than King Saul himself and thus she was doomed, for he had previously ordered all such persons involved in this practice be killed (v. 13).

It is easy to see that the questions about this chapter are legion in number. For example: Could this woman and her craft actually raise people from the dead and get messages for those on the other side of eternity? If she was able to call such persons up from the grave, did she get this power from Satan, or was she deluded into some wrong kind of thinking that she was able to do such a trick? Did Samuel really appear and speak to the spiritist? If he did, this happened not because the necromancer was able to make it work but because God intervened and raised Samuel himself.

Early Church Fathers feared what doctrinal aberrations this Scripture would produce in the Church, so they argued that either (1) the sorcery involved here was simply demonic, for Samuel had not been reduced to a "shade" in Sheol, in which a medium could act as an intermediary between two worlds by summoning him forth, or (2) Samuel was not in Hades, but had been sent by God to announce to the beleaguered Saul his forthcoming fate on the coming day's battlefield. The Church Father Origen, in typical fashion, to cite one other early Christian approach, treated the whole matter typologically. He saw the whole calling forth of Samuel as representing Christ who voluntarily descended into hell, prophesied to the souls there, and had the power to bring inhabitants back from Hades! Wow! That was certainly off the mark of orthodoxy! On the other hand, another Church Father, Gregory of Nazianzus said Samuel was raised, or so it seemed, by a woman having a familiar spirit, so he left the ambiguity in the text.

Saul incorrectly thought he could disguise himself from being recognized by the medium (v. 8), but that thought turned out to be wrong (v. 12). And if Saul was hoping for some good news for all his trouble, he was mistaken, for his cover and desires were completely exploded. The two men who went with Saul (v. 8) asked the medium on his behalf to "consult" a "spirit." The Hebrew word for "to consult" is *qsm*, elsewhere translated as "diviners" or "divination." But that word brings us back to the event that came at the start of Samuel's days of instruction for King Saul. In 15:23, Saul's rebellion in the King Agag incident is one where he, by refusing God's command to leave neither man nor beast standing, decided instead to bring back a sizable number of more select animals (in part) as an offering to the Lord, to which Samuel compared this act to the "sin of rebellion," commenting that "to obey was better than to sacrifice."

When the woman reminded King Saul of his threat to "cut off" all those who practiced her craft (v. 9), he promised her she would not be punished or put to death as the others had, by taking a solemn oath in the Lord's name (v. 10). Whether she actually saw or heard Samuel in a real apparition or not, we do not know. But whatever she saw or heard was enough to shock the liver out of her, and to blow Saul's cover (v. 12). Saul urged her not to be afraid, but instead asked her what she saw. She retorted, "a spirit," which in this case used the Hebrew word *'elohim*. In the apparition, Samuel is seen coming up out of "the ground" (Hebrew *ha'arets*)—not from heaven!_That raises more questions we cannot answer.

Saul was unable to see the "spirit," but he asked the woman to describe what she saw. She said he looked like "an old man wearing a robe," which Saul assumed was Samuel (v. 14). But Saul never saw Samuel himself.

Rebuked by the Prophet Samuel – 28:15–19

The apparition that appeared to be Samuel complained to Saul, "Why have you disturbed me by bringing me up?" (v. 15). Saul had gone to the woman's house at Endor, two or three miles northeast of Shunem on the northern slope of the same Mount Moreh, while the Philistines were at Shunem itself on the southern slope of Mount Moreh. This meant, therefore, that Saul, risky as it was, had to skirt around the camp of the Philistines undetected to get to the witch at Endor.

Saul answered Samuel (or was it the apparition?) with this sorrowful explanation:

> "I am in great distress. The Philistines are fighting against me and God has turned away from me. He no longer answers me, either by prophets or by dreams. So, I have called on you to tell me what to do." (v. 15b)

Saul was in desperate straits, for he fully realized God had abandoned him. Saul uses the general word "God" (Hebrew *'elohim*), whereas Samuel consistently used the covenantal and personal term for God, "Yahweh = LORD." Moreover, the fate Saul was confronting was the same one that had been announced years before by Samuel (16:14; 18:12). Why had Saul not acted in that interim to get his heart right with God if he accepted the truth of those divine revelations?

The Lord had done as he had predicted back in 15:28 to tear the kingdom of Israel from Saul's hands and to give it to another "one of his neighbors," i.e., to David (v. 17b). Verse 18 lists two reasons why the Lord wrenched the kingdom from Saul's hands: he had disobeyed Samuel's command (chapter 13), and he had refused to carry out fully God's command against Amalek (chapter 15). It is true, of course, that over the years God had delivered the Philistines into the hands of Israel (7:3, 14), but now he would "hand over" Israel to the enemy. Samuel told Saul as politely as possible, "Tomorrow you and your sons will be with me" (in the realm of the dead, called "Hades" or the "grave," v. 19).

With his final appearance in v. 20, Samuel does not appear again in the two books of the Bible that bear his name. But he surely must be recognized as one of the greatest leaders Israel had in her early years of development. Scripture labels him as the head of the prophets (Acts 3:24, 13:20); he is also called both a "prophet" and a "seer" (1 Chronicles 9:22, 26:28; cf. 1 Samuel 9:9, 19), yet he also functioned as priest, judge, counselor and anointer of Israel's first two kings.

Sustained by Eating a Final Meal – 28:20–25

Saul was overcome by the message Samuel, or his apparition, now delivered, for "immediately [he] fell full length on the ground, filled with fear because of Samuel's words that on the next day he and his sons would be dead and with him on the other side of eternity. His strength was gone, for he had eaten nothing all that day and night" (v. 20).

The woman, like Saul, was deeply shaken by all that was happening. But she also saw how totally distraught, fearful and overcome Saul was by the news he received, for he had not taken nourishment all that day and he probably suffered from total exhaustion. So she begged Saul to listen to her advice to eat something she would prepare. At first Saul refused everything, but she, and the men with Saul, persisted (v. 23).

The medium quickly got together a meal fit for a king. She butchered a calf and baked unleavened bread, in what could be labeled a typical Eastern sumptuous feast (vv. 24–25). Saul and his men sat down and ate their last supper. However, the chapter ends with the mournful note, "Then they got up and went away that night" (v. 25b). Yes, the writer wanted us to know not only the late hour in which all of this was coming about, but there was more than just the time that was in his mind, for what had begun so hopefully, some forty years ago, a time in which the prospect of his reign was filled with such promise for a new king named Saul, ruling over Israel, had now ended with darkness and the prospect of a military calamity of epic proportions for the nation.

Conclusions

1. What a grim chapter, for it begins by recalling the death of the prophet Samuel and ends with the prediction of the tragic death of Israel's first king along with his sons and his army.

2. It is a choice that is "dead wrong" to ask the forces of death and the grave of Hades for advice when one has for so many years resisted the loving, free advice of a Heavenly Father given so plainly in the Scriptures or dreams and by his prophet Samuel.

3. The focus of this chapter is not on the geography and resources of the netherworld, but on the Lord, who has given us his revelation to inform us as to how we should live so as to please him.

4. What God has predicted in the past holds firm and true for all times past and present. God does not revise or change his mind about what he has said will take place in the days to come.

5. It is improper for believers to think they are in Saul's shoes when they wrongly conclude they have been cut off from the presence of God. When we are tempted to say, with Saul, that we are forsaken by God, we as believers must recall that it is our privilege to cry out to God, for he will be our light that shines in the darkness (Psalm 13:1).

6. Never doubt in the darkness what God has promised to do in the light!

Questions for Thought and Reflection

1. Why was Saul so unsuccessful in the latter half of his reign, while in his earlier days he seemed to thrive and enjoy the power and presence of the Lord?

2. Has God kept some of us going in times when we have made stupid decisions like David?

3. Some of God's saints, like the hymnist William Cowper, have often felt like they were reprobates. How would you have offered help from the Gospel to such people?

4. What word from the Scriptures would you have for all who would depend on the arts of the occult world to guide them?